Counterfeits, War Stories
and Lessons Learned

Counterfeits, War Stories and Lessons Learned

AN INVESTIGATOR'S PERSPECTIVE

Christopher T. Macolini

WORLDWIDE

AUTHOR'S NOTE: The Value of Seized Products

In this book, I use U.S. dollar amounts when referring to seized products. These values are somewhat aleatory in nature because it is difficult to place a true value on seized counterfeit products. In a strict sense, the real worth of seized counterfeit products to a client is exactly zero. The client will never sell the counterfeit products or otherwise generate any income from these products. In most cases, it will further cost the client to investigate, press charges and oversee the destruction of the seized products. Therefore the true monetary value of the seized goods is nothing.

How, then, do companies arrive at the numbers used to describe a seizure? The answer varies from client to client. Some use the average price of a genuine product, which they consider the amount of a sale lost to a counterfeit. Depending on the product, however, this might not reflect the truth. Take, for example, a luxury handbag that sells for US$3,000. Knockoffs of that handbag can be purchased in many parts of the world for less than $100. It is a bit of a stretch, however, to assume that everyone who purchases a counterfeit handbag would have purchased the genuine article if given the chance. That is why some companies assign a percentage of the cost of a genuine product, say 30 percent, when calculating losses attributable to customers buying knockoffs.

Still other companies assign values based on sales increases seen in the wake of seizures of counterfeits. For example, one of our investigations resulted in the seizure of 15,000 electrical parts. The next month, our client saw sales of that product spike by over US$150,000. Consequently, they assigned a value of $150,000 to the seizure.

One other point to keep in mind: Intellectual-property investigations are often plagued by the same question that is debated by narcotics departments around the world: Is it better to seize 1 million counterfeit products and arrest nobody, or arrest the number-one counterfeiter in the world but make no seizures? Obviously, the correct answer is to seize 1 million counterfeit products and arrest the number-one counterfeiter in the world

Counterfeits, War Stories and Lessons Learned
An Investigator's Perspective

Copyright © 2019 Christopher T. Macolini
All Rights Reserved

ISBN: 978-0-5784457-3-1

Printed in the United States of America

Design by Michael Hentges

Published in the United States of America by MIC Worldwide LLC

To my wife and business partner Dafne.
You are the source of my inspiration, the foundation of my strength
and the reason for our success.

To our sons Facundo and Ignacio.
You bring me pride and joy in the young men that you are
and in everything that you do

PROLOGUE

Dateline: Lima, Peru. Time: 2:00 a.m. on a Wednesday.

I WAS WORKING WITH LOCAL LAW ENFORCEMENT on behalf of one of our company's clients on an operation against 64 targets selling counterfeit electrical parts and supplies. The location was a huge covered market spanning an entire downtown city block.

Because crowds usually flocked to the market during the day, the federal prosecutor running the operation decided we should conduct the enforcement action in the wee hours, thereby minimizing the risk of disruption or uprising, whether among the workers, the merchants, their operatives or the general public.

We arrived at the location shortly before the designated time with the prosecutor, six assistant prosecutors and 115 riot police. Using bolt cutters, we unlocked the main door and entered the market. We quickly discovered, however, that we could not turn on the interior lights because the building's power used a password-protected timer. Resorting to flashlights, we proceeded to break into and search the padlocked targeted stands, finding large quantities of counterfeit goods. Most of the items were sitting inside the small shops, but others had been placed in an attic loft, stacked precariously among the rafters.

About 45 minutes into the operation, an angry mob of about 50 men suddenly appeared. Alerted to our presence by hidden security cameras, they had broken through a side entrance of the market and were carrying rocks, bottles and other makeshift projectiles, which they began hurling at us.

Despite the large police presence, the mob continued their advance, picking up and throwing chairs and other loose items along the way. Instead of standing their ground, many of the police, despite their full riot gear, turned tail and ran toward the exits. I wasn't going to face the thugs on my own, so I followed suit.

Still about a hundred feet from the main exit, the police, now fearing for their safety, began deploying tear gas, slowing the mob's advance. The officer directly in front of me panicked, unholstered his weapon and began shooting blindly over his shoulder as he ran – and placing me directly in the line of fire. Lucky for me, the officer squeezed off only three rounds before making it out the door and onto a waiting bus. All three shots landed harmlessly against nearby shops, and no one was injured. But the incident gave me an extra jolt of adrenaline I didn't need.

Most of the raiding party made it out the front door, but the mob captured the lead prosecutor and two of her assistants. Apparently, the police commander felt no concern for the prosecutor, because he and his men finished piling into the waiting buses and were preparing to leave. I caught up with him and related what had happened, but the commander told me he would not risk sending his men back into the building because shots had been fired.

When I explained that his own man had fired the shots, he responded that if I mentioned this to anyone he would throw me in jail for lying. I informed him that if he did not order his men to rescue the prosecutor and her assistants I would contact every newspaper and radio station in the country and elsewhere and tell them what had happened on this night.

The threat worked. The commander, though annoyed, ordered a team back into the market building. They rescued the hostages without injuries. Unfortunately, they also left behind the seized product as they made their quick exit.

I returned to my hotel, packed and checked out quickly, headed to the airport and took the next flight home. There, I noted several phone messages from the police commander, again warning me to keep quiet about the errant shots fired. The prosecutor also had left me a message, and I returned her call immediately. She thanked me profusely for insisting that the police send a rescue team. She said she and her colleagues were repeatedly assaulted verbally and physically, and she had feared the worst until the team arrived. She told me her biggest concern was being left behind to fend for herself, and if not for my intervention that is what would have happened. The prosecutor was angry that the officers who were sworn to protect her had given so little thought to her safety.

Not every incident involving counterfeiting results in violence or a potential hostage situation. Nevertheless, counterfeiting is a crime – and it is big business, worth the equivalent of many billions of dollars annually. Counterfeiting also corrupts institutions and individuals. It knows no borders and inflicts much harm, economic and otherwise. Perhaps worst of all, the culprits go largely unpunished, and counterfeiting is often ignored by law enforcement and perceived as harmless by the general public.

Contents

Foreword by Ron Davis   **11**

Introduction   **14**

WHAT ARE WE PROTECTING? (The Value of the Brand) **18**

PART I. The Counterfeiters

   1. What Products Are Counterfeits?   **24**

   2. How Do Counterfeits Compete with Genuine Products? **28**

   3. How Do Counterfeits Cause Harm?   **30**

   4. Where Do Counterfeits Come From?   **32**

   5. How Do Counterfeits Invade the Internet? **36**

   6. How Do Counterfeiters Evade the Law?   **38**

   7. Who Funds the Counterfeiters?   **40**

   8. How Do Counterfeits Corrupt Markets?   **45**

   9. Who Are the International Bad Actors?   **46**

PART II. How To Conduct Intellectual Property

Investigations

  10. Using Investigative Tools   **50**

  11. Making Test Purchases   **52**

  12. Searching Public Records   **54**

  13. Employing Surveillance   **56**

  14. Using Informants   **64**

  15. Making Trash Runs   **66**

PART III. Investigative Strategies

  16. Tailoring the Strategy   **69**

  17. Quantifying the Problem   **71**

  18. Gathering Information   **76**

  19. Creating Investigative Flow   **78**

  20. Persuading the Authorities to Act   **82**

21. Trusting Authorities (But Protecting Information)   **84**

22. Watching Out for Corruption – Three Examples   **89**

23. Handling Evidence   **96**

24. Alternate Investigative Approaches   **98**

25. Customs Interdictions (Stopping the Counterfeits at the Port)   **102**

26. Online Investigations   **106**

27. Analyzing Counterfeit Products   **109**

28. To Prosecute or Not to Prosecute?   **113**

29. The FCPA and the UK Anti-Bribery Act: Exercising Caution   **115**

30. Understanding Corporate Ethics   **117**

31. Enhancing the Value of Brand Protection   **118**

32. Consistent Pricing and Gray Marketing   **120**

33. Understanding the Role of Public Tenders   **124**

34. Avoid Becoming an Evidence Custodian   **128**

35. Working with Authorities   **129**

36. Dealing with Clients   **132**

37. Building an Anti-Counterfeiting Plan   **134**

POSTSCRIPT   **137**

PART IV: My Story   **141**

Appendix 1: World's Top 100 Branded Products   **145**

Appendix 2: Selected Treaties Administered by the U.N. World Intellectual Property Organization   **148**

Acknowledgments   **151**

End Notes   **152**

Foreword

As FORMER SENIOR DIRECTOR of BRAND PROTECTION at San Diego-based Qualcomm, the chip industry leader in 3G, 4G and 5G cellular technology, I've known and worked with Chris Macolini for over 15 years. He has been a friend, industry colleague, consultant and skilled anticounterfeit and IP-theft investigations service provider. Chris has a wealth of valuable and relevant investigative experience in both government and industry – he is highly regarded in our industry.

In *Counterfeits, War Stories and Lessons Learned,* Chris has successfully used his vast anticounterfeiting, IP-theft and investigative knowledge to educate brand owners as well as novice and skilled investigators alike. His style also makes the book a fun read through his use of actual case studies – real-life scenarios from his vast field experience. Although most of his examples are set in Central or South America, I can assure you his investigative techniques are equally applicable in North America and the rest of the world.

The persistent growth of global counterfeiting and IP theft remains a major cause for concern for any company with a recognizable brand. Chris's book provides brand owners and investigators a reliable roadmap for conducting professional operations against these threats.

During the early years of my career, it would have been helpful to have had access to such a thorough compilation of investigative advice. As a long-time mentor to college interns and new hires in our industry, I plan to distribute copies of Chris's book to each of my staff, mentees and friends. Everything is here to make a brand owner a knowledgeable judge of quality investigations, and to help make an investigator a star.

Counterfeiting and IP theft are big business and most serious matters for victimized companies; they need skilled investigators. A 2016 study by the well-respected Organization for Economic Co-operation and Development (OECD) estimated counterfeiting accounts for 2.5 percent of world trade, or US$461 billion annually. During 2017 in the United States, for example, the Department of Homeland Security reported 34,143 seizures of counterfeit goods with a retail value of over $1 billion. Those numbers are staggering, but Chris and a few of us in our peer group, as well as anticounterfeiting industry associations, have made and continue to make amazing progress, even from where we were 10 years ago.

I frequently hear from friends and business victims that counterfeiting and IP theft are too big for us to ever get our arms around, and there is no value in pursuing investigations or legal action in China, the source of most of these activities. That is not true. Chinese authorities and their new IP courts, just as in other countries, have increased their concern over and knowledge of the counterfeiting problem. Their growing knowledge of the ill effects of counterfeiting on China's own high-tech companies, combined with their efforts to safeguard their IP and products, has led to greater cooperation from Chinese authorities and significant wins – both in recoveries and counterfeiter jail time – for Chinese and Western clients in the Chinese courts.

As with all successful legal actions anywhere, you need to provide your clients with properly executed, well-documented and country-specific reports, backed by legally performed buys of counterfeit goods. Such actions will allow law enforcement and courts to bring cases to a successful conclusion.

Right now, reading and implementing the principles outlined in Chris's book will help give you, the brand owner or investigator, the best chance for success in your anticounterfeiting and IP-theft investigative efforts.

Ron Davis
Senior Consultant, Vice President, North America,
Wan Hui Da Law Firm and IP Agency

Vice Chairman Emeritus
Quality Brands Protection Committee / China

Industry Fellow
Michigan State University
Center for Anti-Counterfeit and Product Protection (A-CAPP)

San Diego
December 2018

Introduction

Information wants to be free. Information also wants to be expensive. Information wants to be free because it has become so cheap to distribute, copy and recombine – too cheap to meter. It wants to be expensive because it can be immeasurably valuable to the recipient. That tension will not go away. It leads to endless wrenching debate about price, copyright, 'intellectual property' and the moral rightness of casual distribution, because each round of new devices makes the tension worse, not better.

—Stewart Brand, *The Media Lab*

GIVEN THAT BRAND WROTE THOSE PROPHETIC WORDS over three decades ago, obviously this is not a new struggle – only an intensifying one. In my profession, as an intellectual-property investigator, I have seen this struggle up-close and personal over the past 15 years, and I have observed and understood its effects on businesses large and small. I have helped protect enterprises that develop and produce the operating systems for the computer you use at your desk, the sneakers you wear on your feet, the polo shirt that graces your torso on a casual day out, the movie you watched on Netflix last night and the music that might be playing in your earbuds as you read my words – not to mention the earbuds themselves.

That's intellectual property.

Why is it important to protect it? The simple but obvious answer: $$$$. For example, a recent study estimated that the world's 1,000 most innovative companies invested a collective US$702 billion in 2017 on research and development to bring their products to market.[1] If they fail to protect their investments, competitors would be free to copy the products and sell them at a lower cost – made possible because those competitors have been spared making similar investments. Despite efforts to protect them, developers of intellectual property lose significant sums to counterfeit and so-called knockoff products and therefore have at their disposal less investment capital for future research and development.

That's the heart of it. Take the healthcare industry. Research into new medicines requires massive investment but pays off in profitable medications that save and improve millions of lives. How much of that research is being rendered unaffordable because sales of copycat medications have invaded more and more of the market, potentially harming patients and shaking faith in the whole industry? The same applies to the technology sector, the progress of which affects our lives in essential ways.

Then there are the advances in agriculture such as genetically modified organisms, or GMO, which allow stronger and more productive crops with less impact on the environment and natural resources. But counterfeit GMO are retarding gains in the world's harvests. In the Philippines, for example, defective counterfeit GMO corn seeds, which the government estimates now constitute about 10 percent of supplies, are erasing some of the progress made over the past two decades by adopting GMO technology, because the knockoff seeds are less resistant to corn borers and other pests.

China finds itself mired in a related problem with GMO corn. Though the country currently bans the use of GMO, many farmers manage to buy genetically modified seeds on the black market, but a significant though unquantifiable percentage of those seeds are counterfeit.

In these and many other cases, whenever countries or companies fail to protect their intellectual property, they risk losing precious funds for further advancements and potentially endanger public health and safety.

You have probably heard more about intellectual-property theft – piracy – in the creative arts than in any other field. The motion picture studios, for example, constantly seek to protect their movies from piracy, a worldwide enterprise in which DVDs, Blu-rays and downloadable files are illegally copied and traded on a massive scale. Likewise, recording studios and their artists fight to prevent piracy of their songs and albums as well as unlawful recordings of their live performances.

Stewart Brand was right. As we approach the first half-century of the digital age, the struggle between those who fight to protect their intellectual property and the much bigger population of those who seek to exploit that property has expanded into a bloodless but full-scale war.

If you would like to track the progress of the struggle, try searching for a favorite movie on YouTube – now the Google of video. Chances are, your search results will yield a genuine, high-quality and full-length version of the feature, offered by YouTube at a modest viewing fee. You also will probably find some clips from that feature, running a few minutes each. You'll maybe see a trailer, or preview, of the title and perhaps a featurette on the movie's production. But you also will likely find videos purporting to show the full movie for free, though if you click on the link it will direct you to a separate website, usually based in another country. This cottage industry has been at war with YouTube for years, with organizations and determined individuals posting unauthorized copies of videos and related material, and YouTube taking them down in response to the complaints by copyright holders.

The motion picture and television industries might represent extreme cases, but make no mistake, you can see the process at work in many other sectors. The same holds true on auction sites such as eBay, Alibaba and others, where sellers offer counterfeit products to buyers looking to purchase genuine items, despite the best intentions of both the auction sites and rights holders, all of whom are forced to monitor these sites continually and demand that any infringing products be removed.

That is why protecting intellectual property has become vital, not only for promoting growth, creativity and progress but also to keep the fraudsters – the counterfeiters – at bay.

As I'll describe, protecting intellectual property happens at several levels. First is the need to protect your intellectual property under the law. Whether through patent, copyright or trademark, the first step is for you to register properly with the appropriate agency or agencies. If not, courts will be hard-pressed to recognize your claim regarding that property. Worse, if not properly registered, you risk that others will register and claim ownership of your property.

Note also that if your company does business internationally, you need to register via established treaty in every country in which you plan to operate. Just as important, ensure that the protection is in place before you advertise or market your product, not to mention before you begin distributing.

Only after you duly register your intellectual property do you hold the legal tools to protect that property. You must recognize the need to perform this essential task. It's the first step in allowing professionals like me to help you.

—Christopher T. Macolini
Buenos Aires, December 2018

WHAT ARE WE PROTECTING?
(The Value of the Brand)

A brand's value is merely the sum total of how much extra people will pay, or how often they choose, the expectations, memories, stories and relationships of one brand over the alternatives.

—Seth Godin[2]

THE VALUE OF A BRAND CAN BE DIFFICULT to determine, but one thing is certain: Nothing is more important to a company's survival. In business terms, maintaining brand value is literally life and death. If a brand's value is corrupted or diminished, the company holding that brand will suffer greatly – perhaps even fatally.

Want to see a quick indicator of how critically businesses regard brand value? Search the words "brand value" on Amazon. You'll find more than 10,000 book titles listed.[3]

Here's an even more direct measurement. It's from a list compiled by Forbes magazine of the worth of the world's top brands. The following companies are ranked 91-100 (for the complete list, see Appendix 1).[4]

91. LEGO
92. Panasonic
93. Philips
94. RBC
95. Allianz
96. Uniqlo
97. Walgreens
98. PayPal
99. Dell
100. KFC

You might not have heard of the apparel company Uniqlo or the insurance conglomerate Allianz, but Forbes values their brands at over $7 billion – about the same as the other, better-known names on that list. The point is that even at the bottom of the Top 100, those brands constitute mostly world-famous names and huge businesses. All stake their brands – their reputations – on the ability to inspire consumer confidence. As Forbes explains, they compile their annual list by taking the brands' past three years of earnings, comparing those earnings with the role each brand plays in its respective industry, and assigning a relative value.[5]

Based on those computations, relatively tiny Uniqlo, with annual revenues of US$13 billion, outranks Walgreens despite the US$84.7 billion the pharmacy giant took in last year.

On the brand-value issue, the bottom line – so to speak – depends on more than the fact that, all things being equal, consumers tend to choose an item because of price. The Forbes survey suggests that when you insert a well-known brand into the mix, suddenly price must compete with an item's history and familiarity. Often, consumers will skip the unknown brand name, even if it's cheaper, in favor of the name they know and particularly the name they have come to trust.

This simple fact of commerce drives the enormous sums spent each year on advertising and publicity aimed at building brand identity. Companies also spend enormous sums protecting their brands – their reputations.

There is another reason. A strong brand underpins a company's stock value, because it increases the chances for long-term growth and profitability. In short, there is no more crucial factor in the health of a corporation, a private company or even a small business than the value of its brand.

Unfortunately, other forces operate in this world to undermine the value of the brand, either for profit or to sabotage a competitor.

Those forces can be powerful because they sometimes succeed. When there is no confidence in the brand, its value decreases. And one of the largest threats to a brand's value is counterfeiting.

That is where my profession enters the picture. Attorneys may register the rights to protect the intellectual property, but investigators seek out and identify those actually infringing on a client's rights. Whether for manufacturers, importers or distributors of counterfeit products, specialized investigators provide the keys to identifying those involved in the theft and sale of intellectual property.

To give you an idea of the scale involved and the pervasiveness of the problem, one of our clients estimated they were losing up to US$11 billion – yes, billion – each year due to counterfeits. This is more than the combined GDP of Suriname, Guyana and Belize. The 2018 Global Brand Counterfeiting Report estimates that global counterfeiting losses in 2017 exceeded US$1.2 trillion – equal to the 2017 GDP of Spain and more than the combined 2017 GDP of Sweden and Switzerland.[6]

In addition to the monetary cost, the EU Customs Union attributes counterfeiting to the loss of more than 800,000 jobs on the continent each year, with a similar amount in the United States.[7] The loss of these jobs affects not only the companies whose products are counterfeited but also the hundreds of thousands of workers and their families who must suffer that unemployment.

Private companies invest a tremendous amount of money combatting counterfeits. Alibaba, for example, recently reported spending more than US$161 million fighting counterfeits since 2013 – and Alibaba is not even a manufacturer but rather a platform on which some counterfeits are inevitably listed.

Fortune 500 companies spend huge sums each year combatting counterfeits across almost all industries. And well-trained, creative, professional investigators are at the forefront of this battle.

On a More Personal Level

How does all this affect the an individual consumer? Say you purchased a top brand-name printer because you like sharpness of colors in your documents and a high quality of print. When it comes time to change the toner, you purchase from a physical or online store what you believe is genuine toner but at a significantly lower price. Without your knowledge, however, you were sold a counterfeit. You suddenly discover that the image is less sharp. Furthermore, the counterfeit toner gums up your printer's mechanism, smearing your documents. But you remain unaware that the toner is counterfeit. Suddenly, you are no longer happy with your printer. You begin to question its quality, which begins to reflect your regard for the brand of the printer. When it comes time to buy a replacement, how likely will it be that you return to that same brand?

Moreover, what if you did realize, after the fact, that the toner you purchased was counterfeit? Would you ever buy from that store again? How much confidence would you ever place in that store's brand – even though they might not be aware that they are selling counterfeit goods?

The same analogy applies – with a greater degree of importance – to pharmaceuticals. How much confidence would you place in a painkiller that did not relieve your pain? Worse, how much confidence would you invest in a laboratory's medication that resulted in someone's injury or death? People must believe that the medicine they purchase from a pharmacy is genuine. Therefore, any resulting adverse reactions reflect not only on the laboratory that produced and distributed that medicine but also on the pharmacy selling the faulty product. Again, if you realized that the medicine you purchased was counterfeit, you would immediately begin to question the integrity of a company that allowed its products to be counterfeited and distributed without repercussions.

Whether or not you have ever considered the possibility that your medications could be counterfeit, the manufacturers of medications worry about it all the time, because their industry faces perhaps its greatest threat: widespread and still-growing access to counterfeit pharmaceuticals online, which according to some estimates account for as much as one-third of sales and are growing every year.[8]

Government agencies such as the EU Intellectual Property Office and even the World Health Organization continually warn against the hazards of counterfeit pharmaceuticals, including toxicity, mislabeled ingredients, imprecise amounts of medication and even the absence of effectiveness.[9]

The situation can be repeated many times, covering many products. It would apply to the brand that produces a battery that catches fire. Or the circuit breaker that fails to trip. Or the whiskey that gives you an upset stomach and a headache. Obviously, such experiences would severely reduce the confidence you, or any consumer, places in a brand.

These aren't isolated incidents. One recent study of counterfeiting called the practice a "global pandemic."[10]

Another hard-hit industry is fashion accessories, in which street vendors sell knockoffs to willing customers across the globe. Luxury brands estimate losses of US$30.3 billion each year from online sales alone. Sport and leisure apparels also suffer tremendous losses due to counterfeits. Almost every well-known brand within the fashion industry has battled counterfeits at some point in their existence.[11]

Perhaps the largest problem, in terms of lost business, involves computer software, which is routinely transferred freely among users bypassing commercial channels. Yet such transactions aren't without cost, because much of that software has been found to contain malware. Trying to save some cash by receiving a pirated copy of software from a friend or business associate could end up costing more in terms of system debugging or computer repair or replacement – not to mention the loss of data.[12]

Many brands have suffered value losses due to counterfeits, and some companies have even been forced out of business due to their effects. Though the harm is widespread – one recent survey suggested than nine out of 10 online businesses lose up to 10 percent of potential revenue due to counterfeiting, the plight is particularly true among small businesses.[13] A recent survey by CNBC featured small enterprises whose products and designs had been copied and marketed online by sites run by giant retailers such as Alibaba, the huge Chinese conglomerate. Though the company regularly polices its online pages and purges counterfeiters, the system is by no means perfect. Smalltime operators can easily go bankrupt waiting for such problems to be rectified.

The scale of the practice is staggering. Just one U.S. law firm specializing in such issues has claimed to have shut down more than four thousand websites selling knockoff goods.[14]

Some companies have been forced to withdraw from foreign countries where counterfeits are even more prevalent, due to the perception that their products have been compromised. As you can see, the threats to the value of the brand by counterfeits cannot be overstated.

PART I: The Counterfeiters

1. What Products Are Counterfeits?

MAKE NO MISTAKE: Every product with an inherent value is attractive to counterfeiters. From clothing and sports apparel to alcoholic beverages, cigarettes, perfume, shoes, electronics, seeds, food, toners for printers and copiers, pharmaceuticals, jewelry and – maybe the most obvious – currency, any item that can be sold or traded is vulnerable to counterfeiting. It goes without saying, then, that the more well-known, widely sold and/or higher priced an item is, the greater the counterfeiting threat.

The most established brands are most commonly the choice of counterfeiters due to their popularity and market share. But that doesn't mean start-ups and smaller brands cannot also become targets – particularly those with new or trending technologies. As I mentioned in the previous section, even the tiniest enterprises can fall prey to counterfeits. And nothing can stymy growth in a young company more quickly than widespread counterfeiting of its new product.

Take the case of an American woman running a small business selling children's clothing online. One day she noticed that exact copies of her products – including one featuring a photo of her own daughter – were being featured at much lower prices on the website of one of the world's biggest international retailers.[15]

The incident lost her not only potential business and time spent fruitlessly trying to get the retailer to respond but also great personal aggravation. The woman's experience has been shared by many other small business owners whose products have been copied – openly and brazenly – and sold on some of the Internet's most dominant commercial enterprises. As I cited earlier, up to 90 percent of online businesses are losing revenue to counterfeiters of their intellectual property.[16]

Just as much harm can be inflicted by counterfeiters at the bottom end of the commercial scale. Since the advent of digital publishing, creators of that modern marvel the ebook have been waging a most frustrating battle against online copycats, those individuals who acquire complete electronic texts legitimately – even those supposedly protected by anti-copying software – and then offer them to readers for rock-bottom prices or even for free as part of a subscription to their services. For years now, online publishers have discovered, via Internet searches, exact copies of their titles offered by pirating sites, usually located in countries lacking effective copyright enforcement. The sites often boast of how many downloads their illegal copies have received. The best the copyright owner can do is contact a pirate website's hosting service and threaten unspecified legal action. Sometimes it works; most often there is no effect.

Pirated ebooks raise some troubling issues in this digital age. For example, online operators are able to steal and duplicate ebooks, music recordings and videos exactly, effectively eliminating in such cases the question of quality, thereby creating a strong incentive for consumers to buy from them. Also, given the lack of international enforcement of copyright laws, what is to prevent more and more online counterfeiters from basing their operations in areas unable or unwilling to shut them down?

Digital duplication is a side issue. Most counterfeiting activities don't match original quality. Nevertheless, they harm companies economically and disappoint or annoy consumers. Sometimes, however, counterfeits can inflict physical harm, such as in the cases of counterfeit baby formula, counterfeit smoke detectors and, even worse, counterfeit pharmaceuticals – medicines that range from ineffective to toxic.

Other counterfeit products that might appear harmless actually pose considerable dangers:

- Counterfeit children's pajamas made of flammable or toxic material
- Counterfeit spare parts for automobile or aircraft that can fail and cause an accident
- Counterfeit circuit breakers that don't trip and cause fires or electrocutions
- Counterfeit toys that splinter when broken or contain toxic paint
- Counterfeit batteries that can explode or catch fire
- Counterfeit fertilizers or pesticides that kill plants and animals and poison the soil and water supply

Industries regularly affected by counterfeits include, among other categories:

- Automotive (examples include spare parts, motor oil, filters, paint and accessories). The U.S. National Highway Traffic Safety Administration estimates there could be as many as 250,000 counterfeit airbags on American roads today, or about 0.1 percent of total vehicles in use.[17] [18]
- Children's toys, electronic games and consoles
- Computer parts, software, hard drives, ink, toner and microchips
- Consumer electronics (sound reproduction components, headphones, televisions, DVD players, batteries)
- Electrical (light switches, circuit breakers, wire, light bulbs)
- Entertainment and sporting events (branded apparel and merchandising, tickets)
- Luxury items (handbags, clothes, shoes, watches, sunglasses, luggage, jewelry)
- Music, film and television (CDs, DVDs, downloads, file sharing)

• Pharmaceuticals and personal-care items (medicines, deodorant, cosmetics, perfume)

• Sporting Goods (apparel, equipment, balls, golf clubs, helmets)

• Telecommunications (cellphones and smartphones, microchips, batteries, chargers, cases, holders)

• Aircraft (the U.S. Federal Aviation Administration estimates that 520,000 counterfeit or unapproved parts are installed in the country's aircraft annually)[19]

As you can see, the economic incentives for counterfeiting are enormous. Estimates vary, but recent studies have calculated that counterfeit products cost global industries anywhere from US$500 billion to nearly US$2 trillion annually.[20] [21]

One problem, however, is that it is almost impossible to know for certain because so many variables are involved. For example, if a shopper buys a knockoff handbag from a street vendor for an impossibly low price, does that truly represent a loss for the manufacturer if the buyer could never afford the genuine item?

Nevertheless, the problem of counterfeiting has grown so large that many analysts have called it a global pandemic, and many governments have established efforts to ensure that products reaching the market are safe.[22]

Unlike genuine products, however, counterfeits are not regulated. Worse, most counterfeits, in particular pharmaceuticals, are sold online and often across state and international lines. A recent Google search revealed more than 40-million links to such online dealers. I'll wager that more than a few have no ties to legitimate manufacturers.

2. How Do Counterfeits Compete with Genuine Products?

Counterfeits not only damage brand products economically, but in some industries brand owners are also forced to compete directly against the counterfeiters. Such is the case in the music, software, motion picture and gaming industries, where counterfeiters market replicas of genuine products – and as I have already mentioned, in many cases due to the capabilities of the digital media, exact copies. So, instead of merely facing legitimate competitors, companies must also compete against their own proprietary products sold by others at a significantly lower price. The financial harm to a company that has invested heavily in research, testing, marketing and production can be staggering.

Take, for example, a Hollywood movie that cost hundreds of millions of dollars and countless hours to produce and market. The production company attempts to recover its investment and earn profits via the sale of exhibitor rental fees and DVD, Blu-ray and download fees, only to have a counterfeiter digitally – and often perfectly – reproduce and sell the movie for a fraction of what the legitimate copyright owners charge.

YouTube has become a virtual playground for this practice. Individuals can use the site's own search function to locate unauthorized copies of popular titles and then employ freely distributed software to download movies to their own hard drives.

Not all of the piracy involves commercial transactions. Many unauthorized copies of movies posted on the Internet are offered for free viewing or download. Nevertheless, each time this happens it deprives the copyright holder of a license or rental fee.

The powerful technology of the digital copy, which is available on nearly every desktop, laptop, notebook and smartphone on the planet, has created an enormous problem. In essence, every copy is identical to the original, which means the rights holder/original manufacturer is forced to compete against someone selling a cheaper version of the title. The damage to the creative and artistic value of the product has become incalculable.

The same holds true for the music, video game, software and other digital industries.

Copyright piracy is nothing new. Its roots go back many decades. Movie exhibitors sometimes kept two theaters going by surreptitiously shuttling reels back and forth between the facilities, thereby avoiding double rental fees. Sheet-music distributors began losing sales with the advent of the first copying machines. Recording studios suffered when low-cost cassette tape recorders made their debut. The videocassette recorder gave birth to yet another iteration of piracy; likewise when the big electronics companies began offering DVD players that could also record off-air. There are other examples.

I recall an individual I encountered quite a few years back in Lima, Peru. He was offering pirated movies across the street from a Blockbuster video store. He had downloaded the movies from the Internet, from a site that was itself pirating titles, and was selling them for the equivalent of US$2.00 each – or half of what Blockbuster was charging at the time to rent a video.

To further complicate matters for Blockbuster, this individual offered to pay his customers US$1.00 if they returned the movie. And why not? The individual had minimal overhead, paid no royalties or taxes and could produce an unlimited number of copies to match demand.

I spotted the individual a few years later on the same corner. By then, Blockbuster had ceased operations in Peru and the building across the street was empty.

The digital revolution, including the onset of the Internet and the fact that enterprising souls can use it to sell across inernational boundaries effortlessly, has merely improved the quality of copies and vastly expanded the market for counterfeits.

3. How Do Counterfeits Cause Harm?

It isn't just the loss of revenues and damage to the brand. Counterfeit products can negatively affect our lives in other ways, including physical harm. That is what the medical industry has been discovering.[23]

Recent estimates suggest that 8 percent of medical devices worldwide are counterfeits, and the rate is higher in the one-fifth of the world's countries that lack regulations covering the industry. But even in the United States, recalls of counterfeits have been rising for critical medical components such as surgical mesh and clip cartridges, both used to close wounds and incisions. Taiwan recently reported discovering thousands of similar counterfeit parts.

As I was writing this book, Brazilian police were investigating an organization involved in the widespread sale of counterfeit, expired and over-invoiced prostheses to the Brazilian government that were ultimately destined for use in public hospitals. The organization comprises numerous medical-supply companies throughout Brazil that act as distributors for counterfeit and expired products originating primarily from China as well as other Asian countries. According to the police, this organization has been active for over 20 years, causing substantial losses and creating countless medical issues.

A major problem, according to industry journals, is the level of skill the counterfeiters have attained, to the point where even surgeons have difficulty spotting fake products.[24]

Noxious fumes from counterfeit cleaning chemicals used in hospitals have caused headaches and nausea. Counterfeit scalpels and surgical instruments used during operations have transmitted infectious diseases to patients, or they caused excessive scarring because they were not sharp enough. Counterfeit cords to heart monitors have failed.

In the area of electrical equipment, counterfeit circuit breakers have failed to trip, causing electrocutions, while counterfeit wires have caused short-circuits and fires.

Your own family's safety could be in jeopardy if there are knockoffs in the house. It could be the dye in your child's clothing. Or the battery in your teenager's cell phone or laptop, which if not manufactured properly could explode or catch fire when charging. Counterfeit brake pads could fail to stop your vehicle in an emergency.

Despite safety specifications, a careless purchase by military personnel could endanger soldiers in the field. A counterfeit spring, for example, could cause a rifle to jam or otherwise malfunction during combat. A counterfeit air filter could cause a military vehicle to stall in the desert. Worse, counterfeit computer chips could have infiltrated the supply chain for missiles or their guidance systems.

Counterfeit parts in commercial aircraft raise some frightening possibilities. A counterfeit replacement part could cause a bearing for the turbine blades in an airplane's engine to seize. Counterfeit software could cause an air traffic controller's computer to crash.

The examples are nearly endless, and in many cases the results of faulty counterfeit products can be disastrous.

One of the most disturbing cases I have encountered began as a request from one of our clients at a large pharmaceutical company to look into the sale of over-the-counter analgesics in South America that displayed the client's brand but appeared to be counterfeit. After extensive investigation, we identified the distributor of the fake products and arranged, through a pretext, a meeting.

During the meeting, we offered to purchase a large quantity of the counterfeit analgesic. The distributor cautioned that he could provide only a limited quantity, but he suggested that we consider purchasing an alternative product from him that would produce a much higher profit margin. The product in question? A medicine to treat cancer in children.

According to the distributor, our margin on the analgesic would be only about US$0.10 per pill, while what we could make on the cancer medicine was much greater. He wasn't exaggerating. The genuine medicine cost between US$800 and $1,000 per dose, depending on the concentration of active ingredients. The distributor claimed he could provide a product similar in "appearance" for about $60 per pill, meaning our margin would be between $740 and $940.

The distributor admitted that none of his counterfeit child-cancer products contained active ingredients, but "seeing as the kids are probably going to die anyway, there's no harm done."

Based on our investigation and undercover work, that individual is now serving a lengthy prison sentence. To this day, however, I remain haunted by images of parents desperately clinging to the hope that their children would be saved by miracle drugs only to be crushed by the effects of counterfeit products.

4. Where Do Counterfeits Come From?

In a word: China. Well, not exactly. Citizens of the Middle Kingdom produce many of the counterfeit products distributed around the world, but they are not the only source. Counterfeiters in India, Latin America, Eastern Europe and elsewhere in Asia likewise produce a flood of counterfeits reaching global markets each year. But not all counterfeits are imported. Counterfeit operations exist in every country. Whether it be an individual copying movies and software, a group refilling used detergent or water bottles, or a factory stamping brand-name logos on knockoff handbags, you'll find them at work somewhere within your borders. Some counterfeiting operations are complex, necessitating substantial funds and expertise, but there are ways around such requirements.

Consider computer microchips, which on the surface would appear to be difficult to counterfeit. You would need to invest in machinery and software to produce a working copy of a brand-name product. You would need to source the raw materials and components. You would need trained operators and a sophisticated production line; likewise a significant amount of knowhow and months of trial and error to closely match the style and color of the genuine product. You would need a considerable capital and human investment to pull off such an endeavor.

Or would you?

Manufacturing a counterfeit chip requires everything I have mentioned, but it is only one route to the goal. Much easier would be to purchase batches of used chips – something readily available on Internet auction sites. Then you would need only sand off any markings, wash them, add new markings copied from frontline products and sell them as state-of-the-art chips. No need for large capital and human investment. No need for sophisticated production lines. And no need for months of trial and error. Damage to the original manufacturer? Immeasurable. If you purchased a counterfeit chip and the result was slower-than-expected processing and even frequent software errors, how likely would you be to buy that brand of chip again?

Medicines can be counterfeited in similar fashion. Setting up a laboratory complete with sophisticated equipment, pill presses and packaging materials would require a hefty investment. Much easier and cheaper would be to change the expiration date on expired batches of genuine medicine. Or, fraudsters can alter the dosage level on the wrapping to make it appear a more potent and expensive version of the same medication.

Counterfeit automotive parts are sold by the millions. They can be highly sophisticated copies or as simple as thoroughly cleaning used parts and selling them as new. Or, fraudsters can change the markings on cheaper compatibles to make them appear to be genuine name-brands.

The same holds true for any other industry where it is easy to refill or re-use genuine bottles, boxes or wrappings. In such instances, counterfeiting requires limited or no investment, particularly if the resulting products are good enough to fool – at least initially – the general consuming public.

Field Lesson 1 – Counterfeiters can be clever

Sophistication might not be a constant requirement for counterfeiters, but a level of ingenuity is often the case. Take the example of a cigarette carton our company investigated several years back. A small tobacco company had successfully copied the look of a popular brand of cigarettes but was having difficulty replicating the genuine packaging and wrappings.

After months of effort, the differences between the genuine and counterfeit were still enough to alert all but the least-attentive consumer. Instead of giving up, however, the counterfeiters located the authorized printer for the real products and simply paid them to print hundreds of thousands of additional cigarette boxes, complete with the corresponding tax stamps.

Think of the problem faced by the brand holder as counterfeit cigarettes flooded the market in genuine packaging. The company saw an immediate drop in sales despite the continuing popularity of their brand.

Even after the operation was uncovered, the brand had no easy way of determining which cigarettes were genuine and which were counterfeit without opening the packages and sending sample cigarettes to their laboratory for analysis. In the meantime, they remained responsible for all of the health and liability issues imposed on them by the counterfeit cigarettes invading the market.

By this time, there was no getting around the harm.

The cigarette manufacturer shut down local operations and resumed selling in that country 18 months later, when they were relatively sure all of the counterfeit products had cleared the market. Then, the company manufactured all of their cigarettes abroad, and they imposed much stricter requirements on their new carton supplier. But their loss of both market share and consumer confidence was huge, and the brand never recovered the level of success and acceptance they had previously enjoyed.

Occam's Gaming Razor

In the world of science there is a problem-solving approach called Occam's Razor. It states that whenever a mystery arises the simplest answer is probably the correct one. I offer the following case study as evidence.

I know of a large computer-gaming company that invested millions to develop a chip to prevent counterfeit games from being played on their newest consoles. Their technicians spent countless hours developing and testing the chip to ensure it was impossible to crack.

On the day the much-anticipated consoles were released, hackers quickly concluded that the claims of inviolability were indeed true. So, rather than waste energy trying to crack the uncrackable, they simply swapped the proprietary chip in the console with a generic processor chip that could read counterfeit games on the platform. They now had a console armed with the latest graphics and technology that could accept counterfeit games. All of the money spent and hours invested in developing a secure chip was neutralized in less than 24 hours.

A Cautionary Addendum

Yes, the ingenuity of counterfeiters can appear to be unstoppable. But sometimes the fraudsters can outsmart themselves. Returning to those counterfeit cigarettes, as it happened the manufacturer had created a product that could have flourished under its own brand – smokers actually enjoyed the taste of the knockoffs and continued to purchase them enthusiastically. Of course, to go legit would have required investing in branding, design, advertising, marketing and other necessary areas, something the counterfeiters apparently were loath to do. So, when the genuine product was withdrawn from the market, and the knockoffs were suppressed, both parties suffered.

Working Conditions

Counterfeit products are often produced in harsh and unsafe environments, particularly those manufactured in third world nations. Counterfeit clothing and designer handbags emerge primarily from so-called sweatshops, which force employees to perform 12-or-more-hour shifts for minimal pay. Many of the laborers are children as young as age seven. In several well-documented cases, authorities have found adults and young children alike chained to sewing machines to ensure uninterrupted production. Workers who pause or complain are often slapped, hit or otherwise abused to force them to continue.

The facilities lack basic sanitary conditions; the overcrowded workspaces offer no heating or cooling, no working restrooms and limited and insubstantial meals.

Manufacturing facilities for counterfeit products are a far cry from the standards established for lawful facilities and by brand owners for genuine products.

5. How Do Counterfeits Invade the Internet?

The World Wide Web over the past two decades has become an indispensable tool for companies and individuals conducting legitimate commerce. But it also has developed into a godsend for counterfeiters. In addition to facilitating the sharing of digital files instantaneously around the globe, the Internet also functions as an international marketplace for the distribution of counterfeit goods anonymously. Anyone can easily sell counterfeit products to individuals in a different city, state or country behind a veil of deliberate obscurity, without the need for a face-to-face meeting and with little chance of being caught.

Auction sites have emerged as a favorite means for counterfeiters to peddle their goods to unsuspecting consumers. Along with offering goods, auction sites serve as tools for the counterfeiting trade itself. A quick search of Tradekey and similar websites reveals suppliers offering to counterfeit particular brands on an industrial scale, allowing individuals to outsource their whole counterfeiting operation.

Other auction sites are rife with individuals offering the supplies necessary to produce counterfeits: components, packaging and even security labels and tax stamps. Many of these items are sold individually and without any trademark, making them legal to sell and difficult to combat. When these components are combined, a counterfeit is born.

Even social media sites have become conduits for the sale of counterfeit products. Facebook's Groups option allows private member-to-member sales, with financial transactions completed via Facebook's own app. Twitter introduced a "Buy Now" feature a few years back, allowing purchases across their platform. Pinterest also offers similar capabilities. Other services such as Soldsie, Have2haveit or Shopseen allow direct sales from Instagram sites.

As you can see, the Internet has greatly increased the reach of legitimate international commerce, but it has also allowed counterfeiters to expand their operations globally – and with surprisingly little risk.

5. How Do Counterfeiters Evade the Law?

Obviously, counterfeiting is illegal in most places, and a majority of the countries around the world have imposed laws and regulations to address and discourage the practice. For years, law-enforcement agencies have worked to cooperate in the fight against counterfeiters. In 2011, for example, Australia, Canada, South Korea, Japan, Morocco, Singapore and the United States signed the Anti-Counterfeiting Trade Agreement (ACTA). The pact was considered an important step in the international effort to fight counterfeiting and copyright piracy.[25]

Then there is the World Intellectual Property Organization, one of the 17 specialized agencies of the United Nations. Created in 1967, WIPO presently comprises 188 member states and administers 26 international treaties pertaining to intellectual-property protection (see Appendix 2).

Groups such as the International Anticounterfeiting Coalition (IACC) and the International Trademark Association (INTA) lobby governments to strengthen existing intellectual-property laws. Similar organizations have been created to bring together companies under common fronts to combat counterfeiting. Despite such efforts, however, in practical terms the laws remain weak.[26]

Today in most countries, if an individual is convicted of counterfeiting or selling counterfeit goods, the penalty amounts to little more than restitution for damages to the company and seizure of counterfeit items. Such a mild response might be appropriate for an individual acting alone and, say, selling the counterfeit shirts he prints in his basement, but it is inadequate against organizations involved in large-scale counterfeiting operations.

Even in countries where the laws are strong, authorities sometimes choose not to apply them fully. Or, countries facing dire security issues, such as high murder rates, rampant drug trafficking or civil unrest, tend to focus their attention on these more dangerous activities, choosing to ignore counterfeiting

Other countries ignore intellectual-property laws outright as a substitute for instilling adequate social programs for their people. During the first two years of his term, the president of one Latin American country called for a moratorium on actions against those producing and distributing counterfeit music, movies, software and electronic games. His rationale was that these activities were helping a lot of families survive.

In that same country, street vendors signed an agreement with the union representing movie cinematographers, promising not to sell pirated copies of locally produced movies or music to avoid financially harming the artists and producers among their fellow countrymen. As a result, the vendors continued to sell counterfeit copies of only foreign movies and music.

Why the leniency? For one thing, profits derived from counterfeiting activities can be enormous. With no research or marketing involved, no sales teams, no advertising, no taxes and no legal costs, the equation turns into a simple costs-to-produce vs. selling price, leaving a far greater profit margin than the genuine product. Therefore, counterfeiters can afford to pay off local officials charged with enforcing anti-piracy laws. For another, generous bribes from counterfeiters, and the resulting inattention, can make local law enforcement more willing to concentrate on drug trafficking and related crimes that pose a greater hazard to the community. Another reason is that counterfeiting can substitute for social programs. In a conversation with the interior minister of one country, I learned that he thought private industry should provide economic alternatives for counterfeiters being forced out of business by enforcement of intellectual-property laws. In another country, the governor of one of the most important industrial states ordered one of my clients to sit down with counterfeiters and come to an agreement. He even went so far as to state that the company should offer the counterfeiters genuine products at a reduced price and make them official distributors. As you might imagine, the client refused.

As a result of such unofficial policies, in many countries, prosecuting counterfeiters usually requires three convictions before imprisonment is even contemplated.

Regarding larger and more sophisticated counterfeiting operations, they tend to reside in countries and regions where authorities are either compliant or complicit. In fact, there is evidence that some countries utilize counterfeiting as an economic weapon against their rivals. You could call it commercial terrorism.

The counterfeiters' governmental allies use the tactic to weaken competing businesses and undermine their host-countries' economies. They usually fall short of this goal, but the partnerships between counterfeiters and friendly governments do enough harm to keep the major economies on their toes.

Each year, the Office of the U.S. Trade Representative compiles a Special 301 Report under the requirements of the Trade Act 1974. It lists countries perceived to be noncooperative in combating intellectual-property crimes. The results of that report affect U.S. foreign-aid decisions.[27]

7. Who Funds the Counterfeiters?

Potentially fat profit margins and negligent legal penalties have made counterfeiting highly attractive to large-scale criminal organizations, which often use such activities to fund other criminal endeavors. Counterfeiters utilize the same routes and logistics to transport their products as do drug and weapons traffickers, and they access the same infrastructure to launder their proceeds.

Authorities have long suspected that counterfeiting revenues are linked to terrorist activities around the world. Evidence of this has surfaced in locations such as the Tri-border area of Argentina,

Paraguay and Brazil, as well as in Lebanon and Saudi Arabia in the Middle East. Likewise, investigators have found ties between counterfeiting and the IRA in Ireland and homegrown terrorists operating within the United States.

Field Lesson 2 – Counterfeiters can multi-task

I recall one investigation in which federal agents in one country were negotiating in an undercover capacity with a member of a Middle East terrorist group to trade cocaine for surface-to-air missiles. The terrorists were using the money they purloined from drug trafficking to fund their nefarious agenda. Interesting enough, the following week, as a result of one of our investigations, authorities took down a large-scale motion picture and software copying facility operating in a warehouse owned by that same individual. They found more than 100 CD/DVD burners capable of manufacturing several thousand copies of pirated software and motion pictures per day. The counterfeiting, like the drug trafficking, served as a means of funding terrorist activities.

Selling counterfeit products has been shown worldwide to be a highly lucrative enterprise with risks far lower than other criminal activities. It is analogous to dealing in marijuana in areas where it remains illegal. The profits are high and the risks are relatively low compared with dealing in cocaine, heroin or other powerful drugs. Yet the same drug cartels that routinely engage in terror and murder derive revenues from socially acceptable pot sales. Something to keep in mind when buying that knockoff handbag or watch from an innocent-looking street vendor.

Field Lesson 3 – Counterfeiters can be successful amateurs

Not all counterfeiters are in it for the money. We took a case several years back for a client that had developed specialized software to protect computers in cyber cafes from unwittingly downloading malware or unauthorized programs. The company discovered that someone had counterfeited their software, removing the activation algorithm and posted the fraudulent program on the Internet for free downloading. The individual who had counterfeited the product clearly identified himself, posting his full name and city of residence – Rosario, Argentina – on the site. Our client asked us to verify the individual's identity and attempt to make contact.

Our research confirmed that the individual did indeed live in the city of Rosario, in the Province of Santa Fe. We also determined that the individual was only 15 years old and therefore considered a minor under Argentine law.

Fearing backlash and damage to the brand if they took legal or criminal action against a minor, our client asked us to visit the individual and his parents in an attempt to reason with him and remove the software from the site. This was before the era of P2P and Torrenting, so at this stage the counterfeit software was confined to one or two sites where it could be downloaded.

When we arrived in Rosario, we found that the young man's residence was located in one of the city's poorer neighborhoods. The house was small, with two bedrooms, exposed concrete floors and a tin roof.

We timed our arrival to coincide with the subject's return from school. His mother let us into the house, where we sat and spoke with both of them regarding the potential consequences of his actions. To our surprise, the subject showed no signs of being nervous or even concern that we had found him. He openly admitted counterfeiting the product, defeating the activation algorithm and posting it.

Even more interesting, however, was the reason he posted the software. The young man told us that when he had purchased a copy of the software, he downloaded it onto a computer used by him and his two younger brothers – him for doing homework and programming, and them for playing computer games. He explained that the computer had been infected twice by viruses and malware, apparently from his brothers' gaming sites. So, he purchased and installed the software to protect the computer from infections.

He explained further that soon after he purchased the software, he unfortunately misplaced its activation algorithm. So, he contacted the company via online chat. The company's representative informed him that they could not provide a replacement. When he asked why, the representative responded, "because that would allow people who have not bought the software to download and utilize, like you are trying to do right now."

The young man countered that he had purchased the software legally, but the representative did not believe him and accused him of wanting the algorithm so he could illegally activate copies of the software. The young man had saved the exchange and showed us the complete dialogue, in which the company's representative became increasingly aggressive in his comments. He told us the experience had prompted him to hack the activation algorithm and post the software for free downloading.

We relayed the results of our interview to the client, who requested that we offer the young man a sincere apology and free software for life in exchange for removing the free download. He refused.

Next, the client offered to pay the young man to demonstrate how he had hacked the activation algorithm. Again, he refused.

The client went on to offer the hacker a red-team job with the company, in which he would continue trying to penetrate their future software algorithms to help them protect the security of their software. He refused yet again.

Last, the client pleaded with the young man and his mother, stating that the jobs and livelihood of the company's 75 employees were at stake. But the stubborn youth remained unmoved. The mother sided with her son, stating that nobody had a right to mistreat another person, and she asked us to leave.

In the weeks that followed, the client saw sales dwindle and profits decrease dramatically. The client then sent a cease-and-desist letter to the young man and even threatened lawsuits, but the drop in profits was so swift, as word spread about the free download, that the client ended up laying off their entire sales and administrative staff, retaining only a handful of programmers desperately working to develop an improved and updated version of the software. Even then, the small team labored under the fear that their new software would be hacked and posted by that same young man from Rosario.

This case illustrates how fragile a brand can be – the acts a 15-year-old individual almost brought down a company operating on a global platform.

As a postscript, our client asked us to contact the young man before they released the updated software and ask if he intended to hack the algorithm. He responded that he had no interest in the new version – unless he was mistreated by the company again. He added that he had moved on; his new computer no longer required the software.

That was then. Today, P2P and Torrenting sites have obliterated the software market, forcing many companies to adapt or go out of business.

8. How Do Counterfeits Corrupt Markets?

Because counterfeiting exists outside the law, counterfeiters impose the same corrosive results on economies and authorities as do other, more publicized crimes.

Counterfeiting is a worldwide problem, but it is far more pervasive in the developing world where employment opportunities are fewer, laws are lax and the money earned from it stretches a lot farther.

In most developing nations, the power is in the hands of few, and nepotism plays a much larger role. It is not uncommon to find heads of counterfeiting organizations with a brother or an uncle who is a senator, minister or other influential member of the government.

The extralegal nature of counterfeiting revenue makes it more difficult to trace and easier to use for actions such as bribery or informally supporting political campaigns. The temptation for public officials can be overwhelming. Salaries of government employees in developing nations are notoriously low, so the lure is strong to accept bribes from counterfeiters, particularly when they ask officials simply to look the other way.

I know of one sitting president in Latin America who was heavily involved in counterfeit activities less than a decade ago and who remains passively involved today. Interesting enough, his companies have been tied to international counterfeiting activities while he occupied the presidency; however he has never been charged, and his companies continue to operate.

But money is only a portion of the corruptive power of counterfeiting. A second and equally significant issue is the related violence. Far from being merely a commercial problem, counterfeiting sometimes involves a level of violence that approaches more notorious crimes.

There have been numerous cases of government officials injured or killed for either seizing or failing to release counterfeit products for which safe passage had already been arranged. There have also been a number of police-on-police shootings when officers have encountered corrupt units providing security for counterfeiters.

The money derived from counterfeiting can be as corruptive as that of any other crime. A few years back, the head of customs in one town in Latin America was enroute back to the capital city with the weekly so-called booty for her superiors. The money was paid by the counterfeiters to let product pass freely into the country. Her car was run off the road and she was shot and killed. Her bodyguard and driver were left unharmed but given a message by the killers for her superiors not to interfere with them. The killers also removed the booty from the vehicle.

It turns out that the local head of customs had failed to reach an understanding with a Chinese group that had two containers of their counterfeit products held up at the port for over two weeks. The following day, both containers were released from customs. Not surprising, the murder was never solved and was attributed to an attempted robbery gone bad. Counterfeiting is big business and at the highest levels can attract as much violence as more notorious crimes. Also, as mentioned earlier, such operations commonly function as sweatshops and exploiters of child labor.

9. Who Are the International Bad Actors?

Obvious answer once again: China is by far the largest mass-producer of counterfeit goods worldwide. Estimates suggest that as much as 80 percent of all counterfeit goods originate in China, but this can vary widely by industry and product. Whatever the figure, no question much of the world's counterfeit activity is promoted by the Beijing government, accepted by its authorities, or is at the very least ignored.

Another factor to consider, however, is that China has become the center of manufacturing for almost every consumer product sold worldwide. As such, it is easy to identify high-quality manufacturing sites and cheap labor for the production of counterfeits. Extending this further, China also maintains well-established commercial routes and logistics systems, all of which can be piggy-backed by the counterfeiters.

Opening and closing companies in China is simple, something which aids the country's counterfeiting industry. We have seen multiple cargo containers originating from different companies in China arriving on the same ship in a particular port. Inspecting the containers, we have found that all held the same counterfeit products despite the fact that all had allegedly originated at different manufacturing sites. We have also seen counterfeiters go so far as to open a company for the purpose of sending one cargo container full of counterfeit products, and then close that company immediately afterward.

No question, on several levels the manufacturing industry in China supports counterfeiting and other illegal commerce, and though the Chinese are the largest purveyors by far, they are not alone.

Russia plays a large role in the counterfeit market, with little support from the authorities in protecting intellectual property. One of the largest industries affected by counterfeits in Russia is alcoholic beverages. In 2015, the government identified more than 100,000 organizations dealing in counterfeit spirits. They also estimated the total number of entities involved was several times higher – though a large portion of the fake branded alcoholic beverages is consumed within the country. Clothing and luxury items also constitute huge counterfeiting activities in Russia, and it is of particular concern that the government currently lacks a strategy to combat the country's rampant online piracy.

Other Centers of Counterfeiting

In Asia, the Philippines and Thailand host large counterfeiting industries, as do India and Pakistan. Likewise, Turkey and Saudi Arabia in the Middle East produce significant amounts of counterfeit products. In Latin America, Mexico, Brazil and Paraguay have seen significant counterfeiting manufacturing within their borders.

Along with the major counterfeit manufacturing centers, there are hub areas in each of the continents through which large portions of fake goods transit for further distribution within their respective areas of operation. Such centers include the United Arab Emirates and Yemen for distribution to Africa; Albania, Morocco, Egypt and the Ukraine for Europe; and Paraguay, Panama and Peru for the Americas.

These aforementioned countries account for an overwhelming percentage of the counterfeiting activity, but smaller operations exist in almost every country in the world, all catering to their local markets. The activities can be as simple as refilling shampoo bottles or oil containers, or they can constitute much more complex operations. The truth of the matter, however, is no country on Earth is exempt from the manufacture and distribution of counterfeit products.

PART II: How To Conduct Intellectual Property Investigations

10. Using Investigative Tools

IP INVESTIGATORS HAVE A VARIETY OF TOOLS at their disposal. Many are similar to those used in other types of investigations, with some differences. In this section, I will discuss a few of the most common techniques.

Note that what I have outlined in the coming pages are the methods most commonly used by private investigators, but they might differ significantly from those employed by law-enforcement personnel for the same types of investigations. This is because private investigators do not enjoy access to tools such as administrative subpoenas, electronic surveillance or other means reserved for sworn law-enforcement officers. Moreover, private operatives are required to identify and utilize techniques that do not infringe upon the rights of those being investigated.

This is logical and to be expected, but the limitations on our investigative tools force private investigators to be at times more creative than our law-enforcement counterparts while remaining within the confines of the law. And this creativeness often is what differentiates the skilled intellectual-property investigator from a run-of-the-mill private eye.

Many IP investigations begin the same way – with the identification of the problem and the subsequent collection of evidence – but each investigation is unique and should be treated as such. Just because a specific investigative approach and flow worked once does not mean it will work every time – not even with the same product or within the same industry. Each investigation should be analyzed and studied on its own before adopting a specific strategy.

Field Lesson 4 – Counterfeiters can be insiders

We were conducting a market survey of stores selling a particular model of a camera manufactured by one of our clients. The client had been receiving numerous complaints.

During the survey, we purchased counterfeit cameras from numerous small stores as well as from two different branches of a large, well-known and well-respected electronics outlet. Although we purchased the same counterfeit from both the large and small stores, our investigative approaches differed dramatically.

In the case of the small stores, they usually bought from a variety of distributors, changing continuously based on who offered the best price at the moment. Our approach was to make a large purchase coupled with surveillance to reveal the source of the counterfeit cameras. We worked each store independently, and by doing so we were able to identify and take down several mid-level distributors.

In the case of the well-known outlet, the challenge was considerably more difficult. The store was serviced by two large distributors, each of whom represented numerous companies and supplied top-name stores throughout the country as well as in several countries within the region. The fact that these distributors serviced other stores opened the possibility that counterfeits could be present in those stores as well. So, our next step was to conduct test purchases in the other stores.

Before making the purchases, however, we determined which stores were serviced by which distributor. We conducted test purchases only from the stores serviced by one of the distributors – but not both. When counterfeits appeared in several of the stores, we could quickly identify which distributor was supplying the counterfeit goods.

The distributor in question had established a longstanding relationship with our client, supplying multiple lines of products in four separate countries. The distributor also represented other top-line companies, with contracts valued in the equivalent of millions of dollars. Consequently, the client was hesitant to believe the distributor would risk its reputation for a few counterfeit cameras.

Further investigations revealed that not all of the stores serviced by the distributor were selling counterfeits. In fact, the counterfeits were confined to about three-dozen stores, all located within a well-defined section of a large metropolitan area. Further research revealed that the stores in question were serviced by one particular employee of the distributor. Given that knowledge, we could then focus our investigation on the employee.

After searching public records, we found that our target, along with his cousin, was part-owner of a company involved in importing electronics from China. We also identified an office and warehouse used by both men. We learned through a credit check (which was legal to obtain without a release in the country in question) that the subject had accumulated considerable debt, in good standing, that he was paying off each month – though the payments far exceeded his income from the distributor.

The evidence we had collected led us to conclude that the distributor was not involved, so we approached the distributor and informed them about the situation. The distributor immediately called the employee in for questioning, with us present.

After several hours, the employee admitted everything. He even gave us access to his warehouse, where we were able to see there were only a couple of additional cameras stored. He handed over the remaining counterfeits and agreed to pay restitution to the client in exchange for not prosecuting. He also presented his resignation effective immediately. The distributor, eager to avoid adverse publicity, made further concessions to the client, including reimbursement of our investigative fees. Our client ultimately accepted the settlement.

In both cases, the investigations started off the same, with a purchase of a counterfeit camera, but the investigative approach, and outcome for each, had differed significantly.

Another Object Lesson

We had achieved a successful operation. But we are always mindful that counterfeiters can learn from their mistakes, forcing investigators to change their tactics.

For one of our clients, we successfully took down numerous counterfeiters using a basic formula: We made a test purchase followed by a larger test purchase combined with surveillance to identify the storage facility, all leading to an enforcement action.

We succeeded with this formula for several years – until our efforts came to a screeching halt. Suddenly, each time we tried to complete that second step of making a larger purchase, the counterfeiters would refuse to sell, claiming they were out of product, even when we could plainly see the target items stacked on their shelves.

The counterfeiters had caught on – they learned our modus operandi. We became aware that they were onto our strategy, so we had to modify our investigative approach into something we continue to use successfully today.

11. Making Test Purchases

A test purchase is simply a purchase of an item suspected of being counterfeit. Many stores, particularly smaller and independent stores, might display empty boxes or old product on their floor while providing new and genuine product when the transaction is completed. Others do the opposite, using genuine product as bait and providing counterfeit products at the moment of sale. Still others intermix genuine and counterfeit products, a process known as "salting." The only way to determine exactly what a store is selling is by purchasing the merchandise.

Test purchases don't require much skill, but they do involve preparation and thought. This will be the first interaction with a potential counterfeiter, so the investigator needs to set the stage for future interactions if the product turns out to be counterfeit. We accomplish this by concocting a cover story for the salesperson about what we are looking for and what future needs we might have.

For example, if a client retains us to purchase blue jeans believed to be counterfeit, we might tell the salesperson we are opening a store in a specific area and are looking to secure stock. We then might ask the salesperson whether they offer all sizes, what colors are available and how quickly they can supply 10 pairs of one particular size. We might ask about possible discounts for large purchases, whether we could pick up directly from their warehouse and whether we could purchase without paying the sales tax.

The answers to all these questions provide important information if the items purchased turn out to be counterfeit and an investigation ensues. Without a well-thought-out backstory, however, such questions could arouse suspicion; they might alert the counterfeiter of a potential problem.

When conducting a test purchase, it helps to think ahead; you might want to use the item as evidence for the police or in a criminal proceeding if it is found to be counterfeit. For this reason, we recommend always obtaining a receipt or photographs of the merchandise to prove that an item was actually purchased from a particular store or merchant.

Test purchases should also contain chain-of-custody details: who has had possession and access to the items purchased at all times. The chain of custody might become important if the case goes to trial and you must prove the targeted store supplied the counterfeit item. Without a proper chain-of-custody report, a good defense attorney could claim that the evidence was replaced or somehow tainted, thus negating its value.

You might need to provide a sworn statement at a later date concerning the purchase. Also, depending on the legal jurisdiction, it might be necessary to bring along a local police officer to witness the purchase.

Test purchases can also be used to document fraud, such as in a case we were working as I was writing this book. The intellectual-property laws in the country were fairly weak – the maximum penalty being an insignificant fine with no other repercussions. The fraud laws, on the other hand, were much stronger and could help us shut down the operation. So, we opted to bring fraud charges against the company selling counterfeits of our client's brand.

To do this, we needed to prove that several citizens had been defrauded by the counterfeiters. We dispatched three of our operatives to make test purchases from the company. When they returned with their purchases, and after we determined that the products were counterfeit, each individual swore out a complaint, providing documentation from the test purchase to prove the fraud. We were expecting raids on the target to be ordered within the week, and that they would result in shutting down the company. But the first step in the process was to conduct properly documented test purchases.

12. Searching Public Records

We often search public records for a variety of purposes, such as identifying owners of shops or businesses, identifying their affiliations with other businesses, identifying assets, locating warehouses and other stores, determining annual sales volumes, identifying imports and exports and studying other information to gain insight into the counterfeiting organization.

Public records vary in content and availability from country to country. For example, credit reports may be legally obtained in some countries by anyone in the general public, whereas in other countries they may not be obtained without a signed release from the party in question. Likewise, import/export records are public in some countries, while in others they are considered confidential.

The ability to determine corporate affiliations – the companies in which an individual is listed as a shareholder or officer – can also vary from country to country. In one nation in which we operate, corporate affiliations were removed from the list of publicly available information because kidnappers were searching the records to identify owners of companies to be targeted for ransom. So, what is available in one country might not be available in another.

Public records can be important tools for expanding an investigation. An individual who sold a counterfeit product might be affiliated with four stores selling the same type of merchandise. Or, that individual co-owns a company with another individual who has been investigated in the past. Or, an investigative target might not be a legally constituted entity at all, operating without a license or other authorizations – important information for the authorities when presenting investigative results.

We might have found through a property search that a target individual owns a warehouse in a given location, and through a credit check that the individual maintains 13 separate bank accounts. Via motor-vehicle records, we might discover that a company has registered several delivery vans in their name, or through customs records that they are licensed as importers/exporters – all valuable information that adds to an investigation.

A word of caution here regarding information in general: In many places, particularly in so-called developing countries, a great deal of information can be obtained for a price. Nevertheless, it is important that private investigators use only publicly available information. Otherwise, in addition to breaking the law, you can expose yourself and your client to legal actions from not only the local authorities but also U.S. and European authorities under specific statutes – which I will discuss later.

13. Employing Surveillance

Simply put, surveillance is the observation or monitoring of an individual or location – as unobtrusively and covertly as possible. Most surveillance falls into two broad categories: physical and electronic.

Physical surveillance likewise can be broken down into two broad categories: stationary and mobile. Stationary surveillance is when an investigator observes an individual or location from a single vantage point. If the targeted individual departs the location, the investigator remains in place and continues to monitor the location.

Mobile surveillance involves staying with the target. If the target departs the area, the investigator follows discreetly to determine where the individual is going, with whom they might be meeting, et cetera. Because of the logistics involved, mobile surveillance can be far more difficult than stationary surveillance.

Each type of surveillance has its particular uses and benefits, so it is important to determine the requirements in advance of undertaking an operation.

Surveillance of any kind should never be attempted by an investigator not specifically trained in the necessary techniques. Stated bluntly, not every investigator is cut out to conduct surveillance, and therefore it is smart to recognize and play to your associates' individual strengths. Poorly conducted surveillance can result in compromising the investigation and embarrassing your client. Worse, botched surveillance could get someone arrested, hurt or even killed.

Even the most experienced surveillance specialists will fail to blend into the background on every occasion. If, for example, there is not a plausible reason for the investigator to be at a particular location or under sufficient cover, it would be best to choose an alternate investigative technique.

There is also the legality question. Before beginning a surveillance operation, you must determine if the local laws permit such activity. In some countries, only active law-enforcement agents are authorized to conduct surveillance, whereas others allow the practice by licensed investigators. Privacy laws are so strict in some parts of the world that even taking a picture of someone in a public location is considered illegal. So, the first step to take when planning surveillance is to determine the legality in the country or city where you intend to conduct it.

Legality aside, not all locations are suited for conducting surveillance. A crowded marketplace, for example, might provide sufficient cover, but remaining static for several hours in the same general location would likely attract attention. Likewise, remaining in a vehicle on a deserted residential street in the wee hours of the morning could result in a visit from the police. Open fields, apartment/office buildings and storage units present issues of their own, as does maintaining proximity to the target.

In Ian Fleming's James Bond novel *Goldfinger*, the title character delivers a stern message when he uncovers Bond's surveillance.

Mr. Bond, there is a saying in Chicago. 'Once is happenstance.
Twice is coincidence. The third time it's enemy action.'

That might have been the end of the immortal British Secret Service Agent 007 if it weren't for some quick thinking on Bond's part and some obviously contrived plot twists. But the point is well taken. Even someone with modest intelligence can spot a careless surveillance operation.

The law also sometimes determines the location of surveillance. In many countries, surveillance is permitted only in public areas, not on private property. In most countries, surveillance is not permitted in government buildings or on public property, including government-run schools, hospitals, parking facilities and even airports.

Electronic surveillance falls under the purview of law-enforcement and intelligence communities and is generally not used for IP investigations. That said, there are instances in which prosecutors choose to request electronic surveillance on a specific target via data collection – be it communications intercepts, monitored online activities, satellite or drone imagery or other types of monitoring – something that will almost always be conducted by law enforcement and should never be used by private investigators.

Surveillance, when done responsibly, can be a powerful tool in identifying the next rung on the counterfeit ladder.

Surveillance can be employed in several stages of an investigation, and not just to determine the location of a warehouse or manufacturing facility.

Field Lesson 5 – Counterfeiters can move quickly

We had been working an investigation for several months, identifying retail locations, suppliers, distributors and warehouses of a particular group of counterfeiters. When we had documented all of the pieces of the organization, including solid evidence of their counterfeiting activities, we presented the case to the prosecutor with a request for enforcement actions.

Having been burned in the past by local authorities leaking information, we set up surveillance on the two main warehouses of the target as the request for enforcement actions worked its way through the system. Approximately one hour into the surveillance, we observed workers desperately begin loading the counterfeit products onto handcarts and transporting them to another warehouse approximately two blocks away from one of their stores.

When the authorities arrived a few hours later to conduct the enforcement actions, they found the two warehouses empty. At that point, we showed the prosecutor the video of the products being moved, as well as the new address where the products were being stored. The prosecutor waited in front of the new location while one of his assistants had the judge sign off on a modified search warrant.

Authorities executed the modified warrant later that evening, seizing close to US$1 million in counterfeit goods. If we had not conducted surveillance while the search warrant made its way through the system, the operation would have failed and our investigative efforts on behalf of our client would have been for naught.

Field Lesson 6 – Catching counterfeiters requires persistence

One of my favorite cases, where surveillance was key to the seizure, happened to be one of the most tedious assignments as well. For years, we had been hearing stories about a cargo aircraft flying directly from China to the international airport of a Latin American capital city. As the story went, the plane would land in the early morning hours, once or twice per week, offload its goods and be gone before dawn the next morning. We also learned that the cargo consisted entirely of counterfeit goods.

Checks of flight logs at the airport showed no sign of the flights coming or going, and airport officials denied all rumors. So, to some extent we believed the surreptitious planeloads to be nothing more than urban legend.

A few months later, we were working an investigation for one of our clients in which a clerk in the target store claimed they would soon be receiving a shipment of new products. The clerk added that the products were being flown in directly from China.

On a hunch, we set up surveillance in an open field next to the airport. We posted our investigators from midnight to 6 a.m.. They watched the airport for two consecutive nights with nothing to report other than an abundance of mosquitos, a few snakes and even a donkey.

At approximately 02:30 on the third night, however, our operatives witnessed a large cargo plane land on the main runway of the airport. They then observed the aircraft taxi to a hangar where it was met by four trucks and about a dozen laborers who immediately began offloading boxes of electronics goods, toys, clothing and office supplies. Within about 90 minutes, the entire plane had been emptied of its contents, refueled and readied for takeoff.

The investigators tracked a large quantity of our client's products being transferred to a waiting truck. They immediately notified local police and tailed the truck. Guided by our people, the police arrived as workers began transferring the products to one of the warehouses used by our target. The police seized the products and made three arrests, none of which would have been possible without the long hours of surveillance.

Field Lesson 7 – Surveillance can be dangerous

Yes, surveillance can be a wonderful tool, but its use in the private sector is somewhat limited by budgetary issues. Whereas law enforcement will often conduct surveillance on a target for weeks or months at a time, most companies will only authorize a couple of days or so at a given time, due to the tremendous costs involved.

There are times, however, when you should not employ surveillance. These include locations where it might be dangerous to surveil or whenever there is a chance the team could be exposed – "burned," as we call it.

In one case, we had made an online purchase of a counterfeit item for one of our clients. We were able to trace the purchase back to a specific location. We visited that location to determine the best vantage point for surveillance. When we arrived, however, we spotted a hazard for the operation: the target store sat on the edge of a large and notoriously dangerous slum area. But we managed to spot counterfeit products from our client displayed in the storefront window.

Our judgment about the hazard of the location was valid. When we approached the police to ask for a direct enforcement action, they refused, citing fear of an uprising in the slum. Without support from the local authorities, we could not move against the target.

On another occasion, we set up surveillance on a house in a residential neighborhood where counterfeit products were being assembled. The location meant there would be no place for the surveillance team to set up unnoticed for long periods of time, we opted for a motorcycle and automobile conducting regular pass-bys.

The tactic nearly turned disastrous. On the third pass of the motorcycle, our operative was forced to stop when a group of young men emerged from a neighboring house brandishing a variety of weapons, including pistols. We had stumbled upon a group of drug traffickers operating in another house on the block. The group kept asking our man whether he was a drug officer – and it did not help that he was found carrying a camera.

Our man eventually persuaded the group he had been hired by the ex-wife of the counterfeiter to check out movement at the residence, even showing the group photos he had already taken of the house. They eventually allowed him to leave – but without his camera.

Despite this setback, we were able to win an enforcement action against the target. The traffickers never informed the counterfeiter about our surveillance, and the police later even followed up with actions against the traffickers.

Field Lesson 8 – Danger can appear at any time

We were investigating a company in a Central American country that was counterfeiting our client's products. We had located the counterfeiters' warehouse and discovered they also operated a small store in the building. As a standard tactic, we decided to make a test purchase and sent two of our investigators – one to make the purchase and the other to surveil activities from outside.

When our operative attempted to make the purchase, however, the counterfeiters immediately became suspicious, asking how we knew about them because they did not advertise and used their store only for long-time clients. Thinking quickly, our investigator said he was referred to them by X store, which we had learned through our investigation was associated with the warehouse. The counterfeiters didn't buy the explanation; they called the other store, and when their associates could not verify our man's story, three armed and heavily tattooed men surrounded him while others closed and locked the warehouse door.

When our operative outside saw the door close, he attempted to text and then call our man inside the warehouse. Receiving no response, he then dialed the local police, but before he could report the incident he was surrounded by another group of armed, tattooed individuals and forced into the warehouse.

The counterfeiters strip-searched and interrogated our operatives. They confiscated their cell phones and wallets and photographed their contents, making note of the residential addresses of both investigators, which appeared on their national identity documents. They asked whether the men had family living at those addresses – an obvious threat.

The investigators stuck to their stories, insisting they had been referred to the warehouse by one of the clerks at the other store, and that they were only trying to buy products. After approximately 45 minutes, the local police arrived, and after conferring with the counterfeiters they took custody of our investigators. It was clear by their interaction, however, that the police were in cahoots with the counterfeiters.

The police brought the investigators to their car where they proceeded to interrogate them yet again. The police also repeated the search of their wallets, again copying down their document numbers and addresses as well as emptying the wallets of money. After another 15 minutes, they released our investigators with a stern warning not to return to the neighborhood and a reminder that the police now knew where the investigators lived.

What had begun as a simple test purchase led to our investigators being held captive for over an hour by what appeared to be gang members and the police – ending with implied threats to the investigators and their families. It was a clear lesson about the danger that can exist in even the most mundane investigation.

As a side note, we waited nine months for things to die down before coordinating a raid on the warehouse by members of the gang task force and tax authorities. The perpetrators were never charged for their IP violations, but the products were seized for failure to pay taxes.

Threats of violence constitute a solid reason why many companies choose outside investigators instead of employees to conduct IP investigations. Imagine if those two detained investigators had been employed by our client. Any identification in their wallet tying them to their employer would have alerted the counterfeiters of the real reason they had attempted to make the test purchase. That discovery would have placed them in further danger.

14. Using Informants

Informants can be a useful investigative tool. After all, what could be better than an individual within an organization providing you with firsthand information on where and how the products are being counterfeit? But informants are the biggest of double-edged swords. If not handled correctly, they can place your investigation's integrity in jeopardy, and they can cause serious harm to the image and reputation of the brand holder.

Identifying potential informants is not difficult. Informants can be someone in the same business as the target – a competitor or even a partner. They can be someone in a related business – for example, someone selling replacement batteries or chargers, or manufacturing boxes, if your target is a distributor of counterfeit phones. They can be a service provider utilized by the counterfeiter: a cleaning person, a delivery service, a taxi driver or a bank employee. They can be a neighbor. Or, they can be somebody close to the counterfeiter: a former spouse, girlfriend/boyfriend or friend.

Identifying a potential source might not be difficult, but approaching a potential informant is a science – a potentially dangerous one. You must approach in a way that does not tip your hand in case the potential source remains loyal to the target.

Never approach a potential informant unless specifically authorized by your client. Note that policies regarding the use of informants vary widely from company to company.

It goes without saying that you should never attempt to recruit an informant if such action is forbidden to private entities under local law, as it is in many countries. Always learn the local laws and regulations before undertaking any investigative activity.

When a source agrees to provide information, it is important to determine the motivation behind that decision. In most cases, a person's motivation falls within one of the following four broad categories:

- Personal gratification – perhaps including payment or collecting a reward
- Revenge – someone who has felt slighted or hurt by the target
- Rivalry – informing on a competitor
- Avoiding criminal prosecution – this falls under the purview of the local authorities, and any informant with such motivation should be handed over to those authorities

Handling informants can be difficult and dangerous, and it should only be done by those with significant experience. As mentioned, if not handled correctly, an informant can cause serious harm to an investigation as well as to the investigator's reputation and the reputation of the brand holder.

Some general tips for dealing with informants:

- Fully identify them. Know who they are, where they live, who they live with and how they are related to the target.
- Photograph informants. Make sure they are of legal age. Investigators will do everything within their powers to protect the identity of informants, but they must know with whom they are dealing. If permissible under local law, conduct a criminal background check.
- Never meet with an informant alone. Always have at least two investigators present. Otherwise, if events do not unfold as planned, the informant could claim he or she was instructed to take a specific action, or that he or she was promised a certain reward. You need at least a second investigator present who can corroborate what was said and transacted to avoid a situation in which it is the investigator's word against the word of the potential informant.
- Make clear to the informant that he or she must not violate any laws or ethical policies. Go so far as to put this in writing.

Even if unrelated to the activity in question, if an informant breaks the law, it could impact you and your client.

• Spell out specifically what is expected of the informant and what he or she is expected to receive in return for cooperation. A word of caution about this: Keep up your end of the bargain with the informant. If the agreement is that you will pay the informant following successful completion of an operation, then you should do so if all expectations are met. Do so not only because it is the right thing to do, but also because if you fail to keep your promise you risk the possibility of the informant going public and embarrassing your client. Also, if word gets around that you stiffed an informant, it is unlikely you will be able to persuade anyone else to work with you.

• Fully document all meetings with the informant, including the date, time, location, those present and any information provided, as well as any instructions given.

• Never develop a personal or separate business relationship with an informant. Likewise, never provide any personal or business information to an informant.

• When you terminate the use of the informant, break off all communications.

Obviously, handling informants successfully can be much more complex than what I have described above, but these guidelines, if followed, should help keep you out of trouble.

15. Making Trash Runs

It might sound counterintuitive, but one of the most valued investigative tools is called the trash run. It involves, literally, collecting and sorting through trash left by an individual or company before it can be collected by the usual disposal entity. Most people pay little attention to what they discard, many times leaving important documents or even samples of counterfeit products in their trash.

Items retrieved from the trash have proven very helpful in many IP investigations.

The laws in most countries work to an investigator's advantage because trash is considered public property when it is placed in a public location. Some countries, however, consider trash private property even after disposal, bestowing some semblance of privacy. This means that unauthorized retrieval of an individual's trash can be considered under the law as theft. Once again, make sure you understand the laws and regulations of an area clearly before attempting any investigative activity.

Note that in addition to the question of legality, as an IP investigator you must learn and follow your particular client's definition of business ethics and tailor your investigative tools accordingly. Several of our clients consider going through anybody's trash as ethically wrong, despite its being legal in many countries where we operate.

Field Lesson 9 – Treasure from trash

We were conducting an investigation for one of our clients on counterfeit laptop power supplies. The chargers were being brought in from China without markings and sold over the Internet after counterfeit trademarks and labels were affixed. We made several purchases online, and each time the power supplies were sent via courier, with a return address to a small town approximately 100 miles from our location.

We visited the address and found a house in the middle of a residential neighborhood. Surveillance on the house revealed it was indeed a residence, in which a family appeared to be living: a couple and three young children. We found no evidence of commercial activity.

Because we were unable to make a test purchase directly from the target, and we had detected no commercial activity, the prosecutor was reluctant to act. We tried numerous techniques, including requesting delivery of the product in the same town in an effort to follow the product from the residence to delivery. Still, we detected no movement. We also tried making a large purchase to see if boxes were being removed from the house and taken to the post office. Nothing. We were beginning to think we might have been targeting the wrong residence.

As a last-ditch effort, after obtaining approval from our client, we conducted a trash run on the garbage left in front of the residence one evening. Bingo! We found two power-supply labels with our client's logo that had apparently been discarded due to an error in printing. We also found a small plastic bag identical to those containing the counterfeit products we had purchased as well as four photocopied manuals that had been cut crookedly. Last but not least, we found a courier label displaying the same account number as the one used to send us the counterfeits.

With the new information in hand, the prosecutor agreed to authorize the enforcement action. It took place the following morning when the children were out of the house and presumably at school. The authorities found and seized more than 5,000 power supplies in several dozen boxes stored primarily within the family's garage. Authorities also seized thousands of labels, boxes, plastic bags and user manuals. All told, the seizure netted more than US$400,000 in counterfeit goods. Without the use of the trash run, we would never have obtained the evidence to support the enforcement action, and the case might have been closed.

PART III: Investigative Strategies

16. Tailoring the Strategy

WHENEVER COUNTERFEITS ARE FOUND IN THE MARKET, and a particular individual or retail location is identified as the source, the techniques utilized to investigate intellectual-property activities are surprisingly similar to those used to investigate drug trafficking. The general idea is to work backwards up the ladder from the retail location to the distributor to the manufacturer or importer.

Depending on the size of the organization and manufacturing location, there might be an importer, an exporter and several other layers between the manufacturer and the distributor, and the investigation could end up spanning several countries and continents. But the point is to stop the counterfeiting at its origin – the manufacturer.

Obviously, all companies wish to prevent their products from being counterfeited, but the strategies behind their investigative approaches might vary.

For some companies, the extent of their anti-counterfeiting actions consists of issuing cease-and-desist orders to alert the counterfeiter that their fraudulent activities have been exposed and are vulnerable legal or criminal action it those activities continue. The companies hope the counterfeiters will heed their warning thereby avoiding entering into expensive litigation or suffering criminal prosecution. Cease-and-desist orders are often best employed against online sites, demanding that the sellers remove the infringing product.

For other companies, the sole goal of their anti-counterfeiting programs is to remove counterfeit products from the market and clear the channels for selling their genuine products. These companies have little interest in seeking judgments against counterfeiters or in participating in their prosecution. They simply want the counterfeit products off the market.

For still other companies, the end game might be to obtain reparations from the counterfeiters – in other words, seek civil judgments requiring the counterfeiter to pay damages to the brand holder. The reparation might pay for the cost of undertaking the investigation and/or legal fees, or it might be a set amount to compensate the company for estimated losses of sales or unauthorized use of the product or license. In most cases, the brand holder also requires that the counterfeiter sign a contract or agreement stipulating that they will no longer sell counterfeits of that brand. This is often the strategy undertaken by software or other technology companies with licensing agreements already in place. The idea is to receive payment for the unauthorized use or sale of the intellectual property and move on.

Some companies might decide to press criminal charges against the counterfeiters for theft of intellectual property. In such cases, they want to see the counterfeiters prosecuted to the full extent of the law, including arrest and incarceration if applicable. These companies will often join prosecutors in filing criminal complaints against the counterfeiters, and in most cases they will contract local attorneys to protect the company's interests throughout the criminal process.

For these clients, it is important to ensure that the counterfeiters are put out of business and that a strong message is sent to deter others from counterfeiting the products in the future. Although companies in many industries opt for this strategy, it is usually the norm for pharmaceutical manufacturers and others where counterfeit products pose a significant danger to the public.

Companies might focus on one, or a combination, of the overall strategies outlined above, depending on their specific needs and budget. Regardless of the company's specific strategy, however, local laws and authorities will dictate the ultimate actions used in a particular country.

Note that a company's investigative strategy might change during the course of an investigation. For example, in enforcement actions against a retail location, authorities might find machinery and other items that prove the counterfeits were being produced at that location. Further, receipts or logs might be found showing that the operation was supplying several additional counterfeiters in the area. And information on a counterfeiter's computer and shipping documents might show it had been selling to other retail locations elsewhere in the country. The brand holder, who initially was only interested in removing the infringing products from the market, could then decide to prosecute to the full extent of the law.

17. Quantifying the Problem

In many instances, a company might not even be aware that a counterfeiting problem exists. They might have seen sales drop in a particular brand or sales area, or they might have heard comments from clients or distributors about cheaper versions of their products on the market. Or maybe they have seen an increase in complaints about the quality of their products from consumers. Any of these occurrences, or a combination of all, could lead the company to suspect they have a problem with counterfeits. Lacking any immediate proof that counterfeits exist, however, the best option is to conduct a market survey.

A market survey can be as simple as conducting a sweep of a particular area and jotting down prices of the product(s) in question to determine if anyone is selling lower than would be possible within the company's pricing structure. If a particular retailer or group of retailers is selling products at lower values, it is a strong indicator that the products in question are counterfeit. It is also possible, however, that those products are genuine but were stolen, or even that they were purchased in bulk from another retailer who was going out of business or clearing stock.

Pricing is only the starting point when conducting market surveys.

A more complete survey would also include test purchases. The client might authorize purchases of only the lower-priced products identified, or they might decide to conduct test purchases in every store. The decision would depend on the perceived severity of the problem and the client's budget to make the test purchases.

It is always a good idea to obtain a receipt from a test purchase to prevent any question later about where the product was acquired. If the seller will not provide a receipt, the next best option is to ask for a business card and have the seller write down the cost of the products on the back of the card. A photograph of the storefront or seller's location is also recommended.

It is useful to have the client train the investigator how to identify counterfeit products. Or, the client might prefer to send all of the purchased products to a location in-house for analysis by the client's experts. If the survey is conducted overseas, it is usually more cost-effective to train the investigator than deal with the costs of international couriers, taxes, tariffs and customs forms – not to mention the possible legal issues stemming from shipping counterfeit goods internationally.

Depending on the product in question, and the client's distribution structure, a more targeted approach might be preferable. For example, if a company is a well-known manufacturer of electronic products with a strong distribution network that places them in large, first-line retail stores, then the market survey should focus on mid- or lower-line retail stores offering the product outside the normal distribution network. The scope could be narrowed further to focus only on those stores located in marginal areas of a city, where legitimate demand for such products is low. Concentrating on those outlets, versus a more general approach, would likely be more cost-effective and provide better results for the client.

Surveying the Market

The concept of a market survey might seem simple, but the research and planning involved are complex and challenging. For one thing, you must delve deeply into the background of the product or products involved. For another, you need to completely understand the product itself – its versions, potency, size, flavors and varieties sold. You also need to understand the production, distribution and sales structures used by the client. You need to understand the packaging and security features. And you need to understand the use of the product, as well as any side effects, failures or dangers presented by the counterfeits. All of this requires a great deal of back and forth between you and your client prior to designing an effective market survey.

Some of the questions that you might want to pose to your client include:

- Where is the product manufactured (locally or imported)?
- What does the legitimate distribution network look like? (Is there one main distributor, numerous smaller distributors or something else?)
- What is the cost of the genuine product?
- What is the lowest price you offer for the product to your best distributors?
- If we find lower-priced products in the market, are they counterfeit?
- Are there different-sized bottles/packages/versions/ presentations for the product?
- Do the products contain any security features on their pack-

aging (features allowing field investigators to determine authenticity and avoid erroneously purchasing genuine products)?

• Are you aware of any counterfeits in the market? If so, have you purchased any, and what size or version did you purchase?

• What was the purchase price of those counterfeits?

• In what type of neighborhood were they purchased (lower socio-economic, industrial, residential, et cetera)?

• In what type of outlet were they purchased (a chain store, an independent store, a small shop, stand or supermarket, et cetera)?

• Has there been a noticeable dip in sales recently?

• Has your sales team heard of any counterfeits in the market?

• Have consumers complained about counterfeit versions of your product?

• Have authorities complained?

• Have any health issues emerged as a result of the counterfeits?

You can ask numerous additional questions to better understand the nature of the product. All will allow you to narrow the scope of your survey to a much more manageable area.

For example, if you determine that most of the counterfeits are found in small, independent shops in lower socio-economic neighborhoods in one particular sector of the city, then you can focus your searches accordingly. If you determine that the counterfeits are always sold below normal retail prices for packages of two, you can focus your efforts on that type of sale. And if you discover counterfeits that are, for example, always sold in one sized bottle, or the caps are always slightly off-color, you can narrow your attention even more.

Anything you can learn to identify the counterfeits more easily, as well as the business involving the products, will help you plan a much more effective market survey. The information also will allow you to tailor your results to the specific requirements of the client, providing them with useable intelligence and feedback.

Of course, some of the information you request might be considered confidential or trade secrets by your client. For that reason, make sure you have a signed non-disclosure agreement.

Field Lesson 10 – Counterfeiters can be subtle

One of our clients is a manufacturer of one of the most popular home cleaning products in a particular country. Despite the ubiquity of their products in the vast majority of supermarkets and small neighborhood stores, the client was detecting a consistent drop in sales. They were not receiving significant consumer complaints, but they suspected they had developed an issue with counterfeits.

We conducted a market survey for them, concentrating on the smaller stores and shops serving some of the residential neighborhoods of a particular city. We chose this strategy because the supermarket chains had strong distribution channels, and our client company enjoyed steady sales to those distributors. The smaller stores and shops, however, used numerous small distributors whom they changed often, always opting for the ones able to provide the lowest prices.

We visited 50 shops in 10 targeted neighborhoods, buying our client's items and obtaining related pricing information. Our analyses revealed that over 80 percent of the items we purchased were counterfeit. We informed the client that not only were their products being counterfeited but also that the problem was significant. Based on this information, the client was able to place a value on their losses and decide how to combat the problem – a problem the scope and extent of which they previously had no knowledge.

We then conducted a series of investigations for the client, identifying the major distributors, and working backward to identify three separate manufacturing sites: nothing more than warehouses where individuals were washing and refilling used or counterfeit bottles. We coordinated enforcement actions with the police, who subsequently raided and closed all three locations.

18. Gathering Information

One of the best sources for information regarding counterfeit products is the company's sales team. They are in direct and constant contact with customers and potential customers, and they are the most likely to hear first from customers who purchase products deemed subpar or of questionable quality. One caution, however: Sales teams are quick to use counterfeits as an excuse for sagging sales, even though this might not be the case.

Legitimate distributors are also excellent sources of information, because they compete for sales on a daily basis. If they consistently lose public tenders or encounter other distributors or individuals who are able to supply the products at lower prices, they also become highly vocal because it directly affects their business and bottom line. Distributors have a legitimate reason for wanting to stop counterfeits.

Other good sources of information are former business partners, individuals who feel they have been slighted or otherwise left out of an operation. Vengeance can become a powerful motivator for providing details of illegal activities, including counterfeiting.

Along those same lines, former girlfriends, boyfriends and spouses can be highly useful sources of information. There is seldom a better source for dirt than a jilted lover.

Field Lesson 11 – Counterfeiters can be exposed by ex-spouses

One of our clients had received an anonymous email identifying an individual who was counterfeiting their products. The email included a great deal of detailed information, including how the counterfeiter stacked his money within shoe boxes that he left on the back portion of an upper shelf in his closet – details that only someone close to the individual would know.

Based on the email, we started digging into the background of the alleged counterfeiter and learned that he had recently been divorced. We also learned through a court check that he was currently involved in a legal battle with his ex-wife over custody of their daughter. Court records showed that the former wife had filed a restraining order against the individual for battery.

Armed with the above, we rang the doorbell of the former wife, identified ourselves and asked if she would be willing to discuss her ex-husband. She appeared nervous but agreed. We asked a few general questions and then asked directly if she had written the email. After getting over her initial shock, and our assurances that nothing she told us would ever get back to her ex-husband, she admitted sending it and proceeded to provide detailed information about every aspect of his counterfeiting operation: from whom he bought the component parts, where he bought the packaging, who did the printing work and even a full list of his clients. We had received more details about the counterfeiter's operation before actually beginning the investigation than we ever would have hoped to obtain *during* the investigation.

After verifying as much of the information as possible, we coordinated with the police to take down the counterfeiter, the manufacturer of the counterfeit packaging and the graphic designer simultaneously. We dismantled the entire counterfeiting organization. Such can be the vengeance of an angry ex-spouse.

Complaint Lines

Some companies opt to institute toll-free complaint lines where consumers can comment on suspected counterfeit products. Such devices often can be good sources of information, but the costs of maintaining and monitoring them are often high. A less-expensive option is a complaint email address, where instant responses are not required. The downside is the information provided is often incomplete or unactionable, and the individual making the complaint might not have, or be willing to provide, all of the pertinent information – including his or her true identity.

Another negative aspect of complaint systems is that often the information provided might be inaccurate or even downright false. Distributors sometimes use complaint lines or emails to provide so-called anonymous tips about a competitor that had beaten them out of a sale or that expanded more quickly than they did, despite lacking evidence of counterfeiting. Their intent is to throw enough dirt against their competitor that the brand holder will begin doubting the distributor's integrity and search for other supply sources.

By the same token, counterfeiters often use complaint lines or emails to provide information against competitors, hoping the brand holder will investigate and shut their competitors down. It's a known tactic employed to rid competitors from the market – but because it also helps rid the market of counterfeits, we'll use any help we can get.

19. Creating Investigative Flow

Intellectual-property investigations, like most investigations, follow a logical flow from inception through finish. This flow generally takes the investigator from a lower-level dealer of counterfeit goods back to the distributor, manufacturer and eventual boss or owner of the operation. A good place to start would be with the test purchase.

After identifying a location selling counterfeits, the investigator can make a test purchase of the counterfeit product to be used as evidence. Depending on the product in question, local laws and even results, it might be necessary to make several test purchases. The goal is to determine who is distributing the counterfeits to the retail location.

Some clients will want to bring the case to authorities quickly to remove the counterfeits from the marketplace immediately. In general terms, it is best to move up the distribution ladder before bringing the authorities on board, but this is not always the case. Take, for example, counterfeit medicines that can endanger the public. In such instances, the best option is indeed to remove the product from the market as quickly as possible.

Also note that in some cases starting at the bottom or a single retail location might be more challenging or even impractical. Take batteries, for instance – not specialized cellphone or camera batteries but typical AA or AAA units sold in almost every store, shop or Kiosk around the world. Conducting a general market survey to determine possible counterfeits by pricing and test purchases would be close to impossible, not to mention prohibitively expensive. But the problem of counterfeit batteries does exist and constantly needs to be addressed by their manufacturers. In such cases, the better investigative approach would force a look at the next rung in the investigative ladder: the distributors.

Distributors usually act as the nexus between the retail locations and the manufacturer or importer. One distributor might feed numerous retail locations and might even obtain counterfeit products from several manufacturers. There also could be several layers of distributors, depending on the scope and prevalence of the counterfeit products. Either way, distributors are key to the process of moving up the ladder.

You can employ several methods to identify a distributor. If the investigator is qualified, and the location and law permit, surveillance can be an excellent tool. Another option is to place a large order beyond the retailer's immediate reach, or offering to cut the retailer in for a larger percentage of the take.

When you identify the distributor, you can begin surveillance to identify the next rung on the ladder, be it a larger distributor, importer or even manufacturer. You can search public records to identify owners, additional locations, warehouses or affiliated companies. In some countries, you can search import records to identify past or future imports for a targeted company. You might need to employ all of these tactics in your investigation.

When you have identified an importer, you can then follow several paths. Depending on the depth of your investigative resources and the desire of your client, you might opt to take the investigation back to the originating country to identify and dismantle the manufacturer. Alternatively, you might choose to work with local customs officials to target future shipments.

Unfortunately, in some cases surveillance and other investigative techniques will lead to a dead end. If so, enforcement actions become your only option.

Targeting Suppliers

One of the best strategies for identifying counterfeiters involves going after the individuals supplying the raw materials. In the clothing industry, this could mean the manufacturer or supplier of fabric or a particular piece of machinery required to cut/sew/stamp/design a garment in a specific way. In the case of electronics, it could be the chip manufacturer or supplier or even the printer making the counterfeit boxes in which the electronics are placed. In pharmaceuticals, it could be the manufacturer of pill presses or the bottle supplier, or the printer running off the fake labels. In printing ink and toners, it could be the individual selling empty cartridges or boxes, or those supplying the contents for the interior packaging.

Whatever the industry, most counterfeits are made up of parts that can be readily accessed in the market place. By identifying and following the manufacturers, suppliers and distributors of counterfeit components, you can usually locate those responsible for assembling the finished products.

In August 2018, following a six-year investigation, U.S. federal agents seized almost US$500 million in counterfeit luxury items. According to the agency, investigators focused on identifying and following the supplies required to manufacture the counterfeit goods. The tactic led them to the manufacturing facilities and to the seizure of almost 20 cargo containers of counterfeits.[28]

A Word about Pharma

Investigations concerning counterfeit pharmaceutical drugs can be more complex than other types of investigations due to the nature of the product and the inherent danger in their availability on the market.

Counterfeit pharmaceuticals appear in many different varieties and flavors. They can range from the simple – counterfeiters changing the date on an expired product – to the complex, such as matching the size/shape/color/markings of a specialty pill contained within its custom-designed packaging. Counterfeit pharmaceuticals can be relatively innocuous – a lower dosage/lower cost medicine placed in the packaging of a higher dosage/higher cost medicine – to downright dangerous, as in a pill containing either no active ingredient or, worse, toxic substances. In all cases, when health is involved, counterfeit medications become a serious matter.

Given the above, it is usually best to conduct enforcement actions as early in the chain as possible to remove the immediate threat to the community and avoid damage to the value of the brand. Authorities are often more agreeable to taking on pharmaceutical cases and working alongside private investigators to follow-up against the distribution chain. Speed is of essence in these cases.

20. Persuading the Authorities to Act

Given the huge amount of counterfeit products on the market, as well as the wide array of what could be called sexier crimes, it is often difficult to persuade authorities to act on IP cases. Even those who are willing or required to act are inevitably overworked and bombarded by requests from thousands of companies, all with similar problems. If you are a Fortune 100 company with strong brand recognition, you will glean more attention than a smaller, lesser-known company. This should not be the case, but it happens more often than not.

Whatever your situation, you need to find a way to persuade the authorities. Otherwise, it makes no sense to investigate if you are unable to resolve the issue.

How can you improve your chances of being heard? A number of factors can help.

First is the public-safety argument. If you can make a case that the counterfeit product poses a general health or safety risk, the authorities will likely listen. For example, a counterfeit circuit breaker can cause a building to burn down, potentially injuring its inhabitants. If the authorities were known to have been made aware of this danger, and did not react, they would be held partially responsible should a tragedy occur.

Counterfeit medicine and food items go without saying – the risk is not only inherent but also likely. So, authorities generally listen when such cases are brought to their attention – though the risk can sometimes be relative.

If the product in question is counterfeit clothing, you can make a case that the material has not been certified and could be flammable, or the dye used in the material could be toxic. The same applies to toys and sunglasses, where the product could splinter or be made out of a plastic that can be harmful if licked or ingested. Counterfeit pesticides can quickly mix with runoff and poison the water supply, and counterfeit spare parts can cause accidents. Anytime you can claim a health or safety issue, you are likely to be heard.

Likewise, if you can connect counterfeit activity to another crime, then your chances of eliciting official reaction will improve. One of the easiest crimes to link is tax evasion. Counterfeiters seldom provide official receipts or pay sales taxes on the items sold – and unpaid taxes are sure to attract a prosecutor's attention. Contraband or customs violations represent another easy crime to prove if the products were imported. Chances are, the counterfeits were labeled misleadingly to avoid paying tariffs and taxes.

If a country maintains strong consumer-protection laws, this could be another potential route. In some cases, the laws are much stronger than intellectual-property laws, allowing for stiff penalties and even permanent closure of businesses.

A bit more difficult to prove, and potentially risky, is a link to organized crime, depending on the laws of the country. Nevertheless, connecting another crime to counterfeit activity can greatly increase your chances of receiving assistance from the local authorities.

Another factor is cost. Many public agencies are reluctant to admit it, but they are often judged on the total value of counterfeit products they have removed from the market. So, if the authorities have the choice of seizing 1,000 counterfeit ballpoint pens or 1,000 counterfeit designer handbags, they will usually choose the latter. But as the saying goes, it's all about how you present the numbers. Counterfeiters might have only 1,000 counterfeit pens on hand at any given time, but if you can show they are turning over their inventory two or three times each week, then the overall value of the seizure can be stretched to show a much bigger impact.

If none of the above helps, you might consider partnering with another company in the same industry. Many firms form coalitions just for this purpose, which can be extremely effective. The counterfeit products of one company might not meet the minimum thresholds for law enforcement, the but a combined claim by two or more companies could do the trick.

Above all, you can ensure the assistance of the authorities by bringing them finished cases and following those cases through to conclusion. It is usually not enough to bring suspicions of counterfeit activities. Your chances of action increase dramatically if you can demonstrate the results of a complete investigation outlining all illegal activities, including all of the players' names and supporting evidence and documentation. At that point, the authorities need only verify the information and act accordingly.

Follow-through is also important. You must maintain continuous support from police and prosecutors during the ensuing legal process. What can quickly turn off such support, however, is leaving authorities to deal with a case without full cooperation from the brand holder – particularly if that entity was responsible for bringing the case in the first place.

21. Trusting Authorities (But Protecting Information)
Trust in public officials should be inherent. If an individual occupies a public position, he or she should be able to be trusted to do the job honestly and in a professional and efficient manner. This is what most people expect. But as we all know, this is not always the case, particularly in situations where the temptation of graft, brib-

ery and other corruption is strong. In such situations, public service sometimes has nothing to do with actually serving the public.

That said, we need help from the authorities designated to protect intellectual property. By this, I mean that private investigators and brand holders have no authority to conduct enforcement actions or otherwise to obligate anyone to obey intellectual-property laws – this is the sole purview of the local authorities, both law enforcement and judicial.

There is usually a long string of individuals with access to the information leading up to an enforcement action. If the brand holder or the investigators uncover illegal activity involving intellectual property, then a complaint usually needs to be sworn against the perpetrator with either law enforcement or the prosecutor's office. The information then must be verified by the authorities. If more information is needed, investigators would be assigned to collect it. When enforcement actions are merited, a judge must authorize a search warrant. The warrant must be filed by the local clerk. On the day of the actions, additional police might be brought in for support. So, the number of individuals with access to relevant information can be quite extensive, leaving ample room for leaks to occur.

In the end, however, the issue of trust is irrelevant – you need authorities to accomplish any enforcement goal. Period. For this reason, my motto has always been to trust, but ensure. By this, I mean taking every step in my control to reduce the risks I might encounter involving information leaks or lack of operational integrity.

One such method is to conduct surveillance on the target as soon as the complaint is signed and working its way through the legal system. Then, if unusual movement is observed around the target, chances are the investigation has been compromised. The surveillance team might be able to identify the new location where the counterfeits have been moved, or at a minimum warn the search party and prevent them from coming up empty-handed. It is never good to have an enforcement action where no counterfeit products are found or seized. It leaves your client, as well as the local authorities, open to potential legal actions by the counterfeiters.

The goal is to ensure complete protection of the information, but sometimes there are elements outside our control that can affect enforcement actions. For example, the prosecutor's office in a city in which we operate is located about 20 blocks away from the commercial center, in a mixed commercial/residential neighborhood. The office is a standalone facility enclosed by a perimeter security fence. Policies and procedures operate inside the offices to protect the secrecy of the information. Unfortunately, elements outside this enclosed environment can directly impact their effectiveness.

Local law requires that a prosecutor be present during all enforcement actions. Counterfeiters know this. That is why, outside the prosecutor's office on any given day, you can see a number of people loitering in the vicinity. As soon as the prosecutor leaves the office, the loiterers place warning calls to the shop owners. By the time the prosecutor arrives at the commercial center, the counterfeit products have been removed, and many of the shops have been closed. This ongoing issue has hindered enforcement actions in the city for many years. There is no way to remove the loiterers, but there are ways to void their effectiveness.

Field Lesson 12 – Counterfeiters can sometimes be tricked by ruses

We coordinated enforcement actions on a dozen targets in one city for a client several years ago by opting to swear out the complaint at the federal level in a different city.

The law-enforcement offices were located approximately four hours by land from the location of the targets.

We rented two tour buses to transport the prosecutor, assistants and even the police. We arrived in the city center at approximately lunchtime, with the shop owners happy to see two buses they believed to be filled with tourists ready to buy their merchandise. By the time the owners realized what was going on, it was too late to remove the counterfeit products or close their shops. The raid netted close to US$1 million in counterfeit products.

Field Lesson 13 – Counterfeiters can be tricked by a large purchase

When working a complex case for a client of ours, we identified a large counterfeiting organization spanning three states and involving several dozen individuals who were selling large amounts of counterfeit products of our client's brand each month. Through our investigation, we were able to conduct repeated test purchases to be used as evidence by the authorities.

In conjunction with the civil police from the country, we arranged to purchase a large quantity of the products – so large that the heads of the organization in each of the three states agreed to gather at one location at the time of delivery to collect the cash personally – in excess of US$100,000.

The case proceeded like clockwork. The three subjects arrived with the counterfeit products, and the police placed them all under arrest, taking them back to the station to be processed. I was not allowed to question the subjects directly, but I was present during the police questioning.

At the station, I saw the subjects begin working the police, at first to determine if they could buy their way out of their situation, and then to determine who it was that had organized their arrest.

After a short while, the chief of the division told me to wait outside in the hall because the subjects were complaining that a non-law-enforcement agent should not be present during questioning. Reluctantly, I left the room and remained in the hall where a dozen or so members of the media had arrived smelling a story.

Approximately 15 minutes later, the chief invited me back into the office, leaving his door open so the media could hear. He proceeded to introduce me by name to the defendants, stating that I had organized the investigation and requested their arrests on behalf of my client. He then told the defendants the name of the hotel where I was staying – in the presence of the media – in case they needed more information.

With my name and hotel location now disclosed fully to the defendants, I excused myself from the room under the pretext that I had to call my client. I immediately existed the building, hailed a taxi, checked out of the hotel and headed to the airport, taking the first flight out that would get me back home.

When my plane landed, I rang the chief and called him out for giving the defendants my name and the location where I was staying. He laughed and told me I was being paranoid. But two days later, I learned that all three defendants had "escaped" from jail.

Nonetheless, the raid was still considered a success. We had removed over US$100,000 in counterfeit products from the market, and those products were ultimately destroyed by the authorities in our presence.

The lesson here is that trust only goes so far when dealing with foreign police.

22. Watching Out for Corruption – Three Examples

Experience can be a hard teacher. Most counterfeiting or intellectual-property investigations are routine, but sometimes corruption can cloud or hamstring such activities. Moreover, as with anything illicit, counterfeiting can be highly profitable, and when certain groups are involved, let's just say they can react harshly if someone attempts to interfere with their business. So, it is always important when conducting investigations to assess the risks before proceeding. You need to take the necessary precautions to protect yourself and your personnel at all times. Consider these cases.

Field Lesson 14 – One crooked official can negate a lot of work

Several years back, one of our investigations resulted in the seizure of several thousand counterfeit products. After reviewing the products to ensure they were counterfeit, the police packed them up and transferred them to the prosecutor's office for safekeeping. That same afternoon, one of our investigators was visiting the courthouse for an unrelated issue and happened to see the defendant in our case speaking privately with the prosecutor.

Two days later, the prosecutor's office contacted us, requesting another inspection of the seized products. Their internal expert thought the products might be genuine. We considered this an unusual request because we had already inspected the goods onsite and determined unequivocally they were counterfeit. We had even signed a statement to that effect before the products were seized and removed from the shop.

When we arrived at the prosecutor's office, however, all of the supposedly seized items displayed before us were genuine. Their model numbers differed from those that had been seized. They displayed markings and stickers placed by the genuine distributor. They were also packed differently, sealed in plastic wrap instead of the cardboard boxes used by the enforcement team to haul the suspect items away.

We refused to continue the inspection, asserting that the items in the room were not those seized during the enforcement action. At that point the prosecutor became indignant and asked if we were accusing the office of corruption. The prosecutor demanded that we produce evidence of such a charge, and if we could not then we would be prosecuted for making false claims. The prosecutor even suggested that the defendant would be called to verify that the products in front of us were indeed those seized from his shop.

With no real options, we departed, and the case was ultimately dismissed.

That was not the end of it, however. Eventually, working with sources within the host-nation government, as well as with the U.S. Embassy, we managed to have the prosecutor in question removed. But what otherwise would have made a huge impact on the country's counterfeit market was weakened by the dismissal of the case.

Field Lesson 15 – In this business corrupt officials can appear at any time

After meeting with the new administrator of customs for one country, we were asked to train their officers working in the primary customs zone to identify counterfeit versions of one of our clients' products. We agreed and arranged training sessions for the following week.

The administrator attended the first session and made opening remarks. I noticed he wore a cast on one of his wrists and walked with a pronounced limp, When I asked about his injuries, he told me he had been involved in an accident the day before while traveling in a small aircraft, but he provided no other details.

We conducted the session without a hitch. When I

returned to my hotel, however, I noticed an article on the front page of the local newspaper showing the wreckage of the aircraft that had carried the administrator. The plane was badly damaged, but what caught my attention was the headline: "New Customs Administrator Crashes on Aircraft owned by Cocaine Smuggler."

The administrator was replaced the following day. Also gone were his top officials, including many of those who had attended training. This is why training should be ongoing and not just a one-time event.

Field Lesson 16 – Never underestimate the capacity for ruthlessness

For those based or living in developed nations, it is often difficult to comprehend the level of influence that a skillful or ruthless politician can wield. We know that politicians in the United States or Europe can heavily influence specific policies or laws. But in some countries, a politician can cause the law to be ignored altogether.

We were working an investigation for a client that manufactures high-value consumer electronics. The client had experienced widespread counterfeiting of their most popular product in a particular country. We identified one central warehouse where the counterfeits were being stored, as well as numerous small distribution centers throughout the city. To complicate matters, the warehouse was located within a secure customs area surrounded by a 14-foot fence and armed security. Furthermore, the owner of the warehouse was the brother of an influential senator.

When we completed our investigation, we brought the case to two different prosecutors, both of whom refused outright to conduct enforcement actions. We then approached the country's customs officials, who also refused. When we finally found a prosecutor who agreed to assist, the judge refused to sign the warrant – all due to the fact that the counterfeiter was the senator's brother.

At this writing, we were waiting for elections and hoping the brother will be defeated in Senate, possibly giving us the opportunity to take down that organization.

Sorting the Good from the Bad

The aforementioned cases aside, not all authorities are crooked, not all systems are corrupt and not all operations become dangerous. In fact, it has been my experience that, even in the most corrupt countries, there are always authorities – prosecutors, police officers, customs official, et cetera – who do their jobs for all the right reasons and with strong conviction. It's just a matter of finding the gems in the midst of all of the rubble.

One way to identify such gems is to ask colleagues with whom they have worked in the past and their experience working with them. Of course, some professionals will be unwilling to reveal their contacts, but most will give you honest answers if you ask them about a particular individual or office: What do you think about prosecutor X or IP Unit Y?

One useful tool for identifying good authorities when working overseas is your embassy. In the case of the U.S. embassies, the staffs usually maintain lists of reliable individuals with whom they deal on a wide variety issues. The regional security officers, for example, charged with the safety of the embassies, other U.S. government facilities and personnel, usually deal with local law enforcement on a daily basis. Likewise, the FBI, DEA and Homeland Security, with professionals assigned to many embassies around the world, engage in daily contact with local law enforcement, prosecutors and judges, usually at the highest levels of the government. Many times, they also have developed access to vetted units, which undergo annual or semiannual background checks, polygraph examinations and psychological evaluations. In the case of DHS, part of their mission is to protect the intellectual property of U.S. companies operating overseas. That makes their people excellent sources of recommendations about local authorities.

What happens, however, if you are working in a jurisdiction where there is no embassy presence and a limited presence of other companies? In such cases, you must find the honest authorities on your own.

When dealing with the authorities, as in dealing with everybody in all walks of life, it comes down to identifying what motivates them and then playing to that motivation – if possible. Obviously, if a person's motivation is money, then you would be hard-pressed to find a way to persuade them legally and ethically to assist you. But in some cases, their motivation might derive from other areas.

If their motivation is a sense of duty, for example, then it should be easy to exploit. Most officials hold jobs that, at some level, they want to perform well. Police officers were attracted by the desire to protect and serve. Prosecutors want to punish those that break the law. Judges want to render fair judgments. And so on – at least when they started their careers. Even if these motivations have waned over the years or have been weakened by cynicism, corruption or other factors, the original principles remain embedded within the individuals and can be used to your advantage.

If an individual's motivation is winning a better position or a change of location, you could be in a position to assist. A word to their supervisor following a large seizure can go a long way to making the individual look good. The same is true for a letter of commendation or a plaque thanking them for their assistance.

Sometimes, it is as easy as identifying a person's motivation for going to work each day, and playing to that factor.

Most important, in dealing with authorities you must demonstrate at all times that your personal ethics are of the highest standard. Under no circumstances allow this to be changed. If an authority mentions the cost of conducting an enforcement action, you can sympathize but then clearly state that you cannot provide any funds because doing so would violate U.S. and U.K. laws. If a police detective suggests that an illegal or sketchy investigative approach should be employed, you should immediately object and indicate that you will have to withdraw from the investigation if the operation is not completely clean.

If a prosecutor suggests bringing along samples of counterfeit product on an enforcement action, in case none are found at the time of the raid, you should refuse and remove yourself from the action. Make it clear to the authority that there is no wiggle room regarding your ethical standards. If the authority understands clearly that you will not be corrupted, then they will be forced to play it straight. If, on the other hand, you ever show signs of considering such proposals, even if you eventually refuse, you will have lost the battle.

It is often easier to deal with these situations as an outsider. A foreigner who does not live or work in the area is usually better able to persuade the authorities to perform honestly than a local, someone who is expected to play by the local customs such as paying bribes or not questioning the decisions of the authorities no matter how errant. Obviously, it's a huge advantage if you understand the language and are aware of the local idiosyncrasies.

Problems don't always arrive at the hands of local authorities, however. Along with making sure that all of your client's products are properly registered, you need to ensure that their operations are above board and in accordance with laws and regulations. Failure to do so can result in a disaster for the company and its reputation.

Field Lesson 17 – Counterfeiters often leave paper trails

When a major manufacturer of electronic goods hired us to investigate counterfeit activity, our efforts revealed that fake products were being imported from China without any branding. The labels were then affixed in the destination country. We exposed the entire organization, including the importers and members of the distribution chain alike. Authorities then conducted a raid and seized products valued at almost US$500,000.

In the raid, authorities also seized stacks of documents listing their supplier, bills of lading, customs forms and other shipping documents. By analyzing the documents, we were able to extend our investigation to China and pursue the manufacturer there. We also learned they were importing the items not identified as finished products but rather as electrical parts, saving considerable import taxes.

We then approached the local customs officials and informed them about our discovery, hoping to persuade them to stop the counterfeit products at the port. We shared what we had learned from the seized documents and asked that they begin inspecting all products arriving from China listed as electrical parts under the pertinent customs declaration codes.

Several weeks later, we received a call from customs. They told us they had opened a container identified as electrical parts and, sure enough, the container held counterfeit products of both our client's brand as well as a competing brand. After reviewing and deeming the products to be counterfeit, customs seized the items.

A few more weeks passed, and we again received a call from customs relating a similar situation. Though this review revealed the products to be genuine, the importer turned out to be our client, who apparently made a habit of "mis-declaring" the items to reduce the tariffs paid.

The officials filed a complaint, and the following day the country manager for our client was arrested on customs and tax charges. He was eventually released, and the company escaped further legal jeopardy by paying a fine. But the damage to the brand and their reputation in-country had been done.

So, before even thinking about requesting assistance from the authorities to protect your client's brand, be sure their business practices are in order and in accordance with all local laws and regulations.

23. Handling Evidence

U.S. and European law-enforcement agencies have established strict procedures for handling evidence. But the practices are not universal. In some countries, evidence is often thrown into plastic bags or boxes and transported back to the police station or prosecutor's office for processing, places where they could easily be contaminated or subjected to tampering. To avoid such situations, when you participate in enforcement actions in countries with, shall we say, informal evidence-gathering guidelines, you must establish internal protocols, the most basic of which would include:

• Photographing all seized items from as many angles as possible before transporting. Doing so will allow you to compare the images with the products presented to you if you ever need to reverify or testify about them.

• Signing and dating all items. This clearly indicates you were present at the seizure operation and that the products were the ones you verified as counterfeit. Yes, it is possible that your signature and the date could be forged and placed on other boxes, but the amount of work involved would likely preclude the task as a viable option for someone trying to beat the system.

• Maintaining an evidence log of all items seized with as much detail as possible, including make, model and quantities. Ideally, include serial numbers on the evidence log, but when thousands of products are involved and time is limited, this might not be practical. Photographing serial numbers can be an alternative, but again, depending on the quantities involved, it might not be practical.

In our firm, we have established these protocols as absolute requirements, and we disclose them to the prosecutor prior to any enforcement action. If the prosecutor does not agree to accept our procedures in advance, then we refuse to participate in the enforcement action and will not authenticate the products.

Since we instituted our internal protocols, we have never experienced another verification issue regarding items seized during enforcement actions.

Field Lesson 18 – Documentation is essential

Following a successful raid where we seized almost 2,000 counterfeit electrical parts, we were called into the prosecutor's office to authenticate the products formally. According to the prosecutor, the defendant's attorney had provided copies of documents purportedly issued by our client detailing the purchase of the seized products through an authorized distributor in China.

Before being shown the products, we presented photos taken at the scene of the raid showing the seized items with our signatures and the date. The authorities excused themselves, asking us to wait in the lobby. Half-an-hour later, the prosecutor's assistant returned, informing us that the defendant's attorney had withdrawn his objection and agreed to accept our initial authentication.

When we asked to see the documents that had allegedly been provided by our client's authorized distributor, the assistant refused, stating that the defendant's attorney had taken the document with him, and no copies were left on file.

What could have resulted in a disaster for our client resulted in a win, thanks to the process we had put in place to ensure no foul play.

24. Alternate Investigative Approaches

The principal focus of your investigation is intellectual-property violations, and in most cases that is the legal area you will exploit. But sometimes it can be much more effective to use other laws to go after counterfeiters. There are contraband and tax-evasion laws that can be applied to those selling counterfeit products, for examples.

There also are the fraud statutes. Anytime a consumer believes he or she is purchasing a genuine product but is being sold a knock-off, a country's fraud laws can apply. An even stronger case arises when a government agency purchases a counterfeit. In most jurisdictions, this constitutes fraud against the government. We have witnessed several cases in which a prosecutor or local law enforcement has been the victim of fraudsters, and those cases resulted in swift and decisive action by the authorities.

Field Lesson 19 – Training law enforcement is worth the effort

We had just completed training a group of law-enforcement officials in a particular city for one of our clients. Approximately two hours after the training concluded, we received a call from the unit chief; he was more than a little upset. He had returned to his office following the training and decided to check some products from our client's brand that had been delivered to his office the week before. Much to his surprise, the items were counterfeit. The chief then went to the police central warehouse and inspected all of the similar products in stock. They were counterfeit as well.

The officer immediately contacted the prosecutor, who agreed to move swiftly, conducting enforcement actions on the supplier's warehouse that same afternoon. The action resulted in the seizure of more than a thousand counterfeit products.

We were called in to examine the seized products, which we found to be counterfeit. Following discussions with the prosecutor, the supplier was charged with both intellectual-property violations and fraud against the government, greatly enhancing the possible penalties involved.

Field Lesson 20 – Using fraud laws can be effective

We had identified products delivered to a government agency via public tender at prices significantly below the genuine articles. We reached out to the newly assigned Prosecutor for Economic Crimes and Anti-Corruption. The prosecutor was eager to make a splash in his new role, so he ordered an inspection of the products already in stock.

After we determined that the products were counterfeit, he seized them in place and ordered the entity in charge of overseeing the public tenders to provide a list of all government agencies that had received products from the supplier during the past 90 days.

The prosecutor then asked us to authenticate numerous additional products held at several government facilities throughout the city, all of which turned out to be counterfeit. He charged the supplier with defrauding the government and barred them from participating in public tenders for 10 years. So, government fraud charges can be an effective tool for combatting IP crimes.

Field Lesson 21 – Using peripheral laws can also be effective

Enforcement actions taken repeatedly against multiple stores in a shopping area had resulted only in the shops opening back up the following afternoon under different names. The practice forced us to adopt an alternate approach.

We persuaded the authorities to conduct an enforcement action the first week in December to help suppress the number of counterfeits purchased over the holiday season. But instead of conducting the usual raid, we also asked the prosecutor to invite tax authorities, building inspectors and fire inspectors.

Authorities did seize plenty of counterfeit items, but the real stars of the show were the inspectors. They determined, for example, that there were not enough restrooms in the shopping area to service the clientele. They also closed down several small cafés lacking the proper licensing. Further, the inspectors found that the stairs were being used as collection areas for the daily trash, blocking potential fire escapes. The action closed the shopping center until the owners completed the required repairs. The inspectors scheduled the follow-up inspection for mid-January, effectively shutting down the counterfeit hotbed for the entire holiday season.

True, counterfeiters are known for their ingenuity, but they don't hold exclusive rights to creativity. Sometimes, the investigative side rises to the challenge.

Alternate laws can be helpful, but so can alternate investigative approaches.

Field Lesson 22 – Catching counterfeiters by catching their couriers

While working a case for a client a few years back in a large city, we were experiencing difficulty locating the warehouse where the counterfeits were stockpiled. The counterfeiter we were tracking operated only online and delivered the merchandise via motorcycle messenger.

Our attempts to identify the individual online likewise had stymied us.

We made several undercover purchases, but each had been delivered by a different motorcycle messenger. We tried eliciting information from the messengers, unsuccessfully. We thought about following one of the messengers back to the subject's warehouse, but we determined that tailing him in this large metropolis would be extremely challenging, not to mention that the messenger likely would continue on his delivery routes and not return to the warehouse that day. So, we devised a plan to make the counterfeiter change his method of operation.

We made several more purchases to gain the counterfeiter's trust then placed a large order to be delivered on a Friday in the late afternoon. The volume of the order precluded delivery by one or even two messengers, so we set up surveillance on the delivery location and waited.

At the agreed-upon time, a small van appeared. The driver got out and rang the bell. We did not answer. After repeated tries, the driver contacted the counterfeiter by cellphone for instructions. The counterfeiter, in turn, called our agent, who explained that he had been involved in an automobile accident on the other side of town and was now at the hospital waiting to be seen. Our agent apologized profusely and asked that the delivery be rescheduled for the following Monday.

Unable to deliver the products, the van driver had no other choice but to return to the warehouse. Our surveillance team tailed the van and found the counterfeiter's location, a large warehouse piled high with counterfeit items displaying our client's brand, along with a smaller quantity of merchandise from a competitor's brand.

Based on our evidence, we obtained a search warrant, which led to the largest seizure of counterfeits of our client's brand ever in that country.

25. Customs Interdictions
(Stopping the Counterfeits at the Port)

If the infringing products – or even parts of the infringing products – are imported, stopping counterfeits before they enter the country can be an effective way of stemming their sales in a particular market. After all, if the products cannot get into the country, they cannot be sold.

Customs seizures constitute an important component of any anti-counterfeiting program. Seizures, when conducted successfully, are usually large and cost-effective because they eliminate the need to conduct investigations, surveillance and test purchases, among other activities. The only real cost usually involves training the authorities – in particular the customs inspectors.

This is a logical approach, though the sheer volume of items entering a customs zone on a daily basis is enormous, and no country has the time and resources to inspect it all. Further, no customs agent can be sufficiently trained to identify counterfeit products of every brand and model. So, without support from the brand, customs interdictions are usually hit or miss, with miss being the norm.

Running a successful interdiction operation involves intelligence-based targeting, constant training and persistence.

By intelligence-based targeting, I mean selecting specific shipments to be inspected by the authorities. Most countries require import documentation to be filed at the port several days in advance of a cargo's arrival. This allows customs officials to review the documents in advance to determine if the declared items or the transporters are suspicious. In general, customs is principally interested in identifying drugs, weapons and other contraband entering and, in some cases, exiting the country.

Even though counterfeit products fall under the category of contraband, they usually are not the primary focus of customs inspectors. Therefore, it is in the brand holder's interest to raise officials' awareness about counterfeit products. One way is by conducting their own review of import documents and alerting the authorities any anomalies.

It is not as difficult as it might sound. Import documentation is open-source information in many countries – though confidential in some. In countries where it is considered a matter of public record, private citizens can tap into import records to search the incoming shipments. These searches can be filtered by importer, country of origin, category of products, value of products and other categories, allowing the brand holder to search for possible infringing material. Services such as ImportGenius and Panjiva offer access to these documents as well.

Though import documents seldom identify the brand or model of a product being imported, searches by specific categories can narrow the field significantly. You can further narrow the results by searching against known importers or brokers, countries of origin, specific destination cities or other criteria. Whenever you can whittle down the information enough to select specific targets, you might, perhaps more easily, be able to persuade the customs authorities to inspect a given cargo.

Also as mentioned, some countries don't designate import documents as public information. An option in such cases is to join forces with customs to help them review the documentation in question. I know of several companies that will pay a part-time or full-time contractor to work side by side with customs, searching import documents for suspect cargo. Yes, the contractor's primary task is to search for the individuals counterfeiting the client's products, but the contractors will often advise customs when they see other suspicious shipments. It's a win-win. Customs receives a much-needed extra hand, while the client gains access to valuable targeting information.

Along with reviewing documentation, customs employees need constant training. There is no way inspectors can identify all counterfeit products by all brands; they will only maintain focus on a few brands at a time. Logic dictates that their focus will be on brands for which they have been trained. Therefore, constant and repeated training is essential, which should lead to their watching closely the brand or brands belonging to your client.

Field Lesson 23 – When counterfeits outnumber the genuine

A client that manufactures consumer batteries asked us to help with a counterfeit issue they were experiencing in a particular country. According to the client, the quantity of counterfeits went from almost non-existent to flooding the market over a period of six months. The problem became so massive that the client suspected there were more counterfeits than genuine products in that market.

Our quick review of the local battery retail market revealed that the genuine distribution network was so wide that a market survey or test-purchases would not prove productive – after all, batteries were commonly sold at every little mom-and-pop store on every corner throughout the country, in addition to the mid-sized and large retailers. Likewise, working backward from the retail level to try to identify major distributors would also be fruitless.

The client, meanwhile, had identified China as the

country of manufacture for the counterfeit batteries, something that allowed us to develop an effective anti-counterfeiting plan.

Our first step was to begin pulling import records from the past year, concentrating on batteries being shipped from China. We also watched for batteries originating from other countries in case they were being transshipped from China via a third location. When we had collected all of the records, we subtracted shipments handled through our client's official distribution channels. What we had left were imports from our client's competitors, independent importers and the counterfeiters.

Further analysis of the documents allowed us to weed out the imports from legitimate competitors, which tended to be large shipments on a regular schedule, imported through well-known logistics companies and with detailed paperwork. That left us with the counterfeiters and any independent importers.

We studied the remaining documents and identified three importers bringing batteries into the country – two on a somewhat sporadic basis, with the third importing substantial quantities over the past eight months.

We identified what we believed to be the suspect importer, so we now could devise options for our next investigative step. On the one hand, we could conduct records searches and surveillance on the importer to attempt to identify their clients, warehouses, vehicles, et cetera, and then bring in law enforcement. Or, we could work directly with customs to attempt to stop the shipments while they were still in port. We chose the latter.

We contacted the director of enforcement for the local customs agency and presented our findings. The director agreed to work with us and identified an inbound shipment from our target set to arrive the following week. The director advised that he would contact us as soon as the shipment hit the port.

He indeed did contact us the next week and informed us the shipment was arriving the following day. He asked us to be present when the shipment was inspected in order to authenticate any of our client's products. Sure enough, when authorities inspected the shipment, they found tens of thousands of counterfeit batteries of our client's brand. They also found a similar quantity of a competitor's brand, and the competitor might not have even realized the extent of their own problem in the country.

Following the successful seizure, the director asked that we provide product-ID training to the customs inspectors, which would allow them to authenticate suspicious shipments on their own.

Over the next two months, we worked closely with customs to identify and inspect suspect shipments, and our efforts paid off. Customs conducted three more seizures for our client before the counterfeiters changed their strategy to mislabeling their manifests, changing their importers and reducing their shipment sizes. Counterfeits of our client's products are still available in that country, but the quantities and availability have been greatly reduced, and we continue our efforts to reduce them even further.

26. Online Investigations

Much more so than traditional brick-and-mortar stores, the Internet provides a global platform for selling and distributing counterfeit products to markets, with a greater ability to conceal identity. Given this newly emerged reality, online investigations have become an important part of the overall anti-counterfeiting strategy.

Fortunately, many tools and services are available that allow you to scan Internet marketplaces in search of counterfeit products offered online. Such assets include websites, online marketplaces, search engines, social media and apps. You can use them to search specific geographical areas, types of platforms and languages. You can search for a specific brand, product or industry. You can specify variables such as price, quantities and models. You can learn how long a product has been listed, how many products have been sold and general information about the seller. You can even find or set up automatic responses or triggers, such as site-takedown requests to platform managers or cease-and-desist letters to sellers.

All are excellent tools and can greatly help stem the sale of counterfeit products, though they usually do not identify sellers or provide a physical address from where the suspects are selling beyond what they provide to the platform.

So, online investigations can be used to enhance the protection of the brand, but in more cases than not, on-the-ground investigators will need to be utilized to seize the infringing products and remove them from the market.

Field Lesson 24 – Online counterfeiters can be slippery

One of our clients reported a target offering counterfeit products on a popular e-commerce website. The website proved responsive to take-down notices sent by our client, but every time they shut down the account, it would pop up again a few days later under a different name and format, and offering the same counterfeit products. The seller also ignored cease-and-desist messages. The cycle had repeated more than a dozen times before the client contacted us.

We began by making a test purchase from the target, an action which confirmed that the products delivered were counterfeit. The seller provided a bogus address, free delivery service and a telephone number that we discovered had been assigned to a prepaid, unregistered cell phone – though the area code was for the vicinity of the city posted on the site.

We then contacted the seller directly, offering to purchase 100 products that were bulky in size, explaining that we needed them delivered within 24 hours. We further offered to retrieve the products from the seller directly if they would provide us with an address, but they refused. They did state, however, that it would take the full 24 hours to deliver the products because they would be shipped from a city approximately 400 kilometers from our delivery location. They further stated that, due to the quantity, they would be sending a truck with the products instead of their normal courier service, and they would expect a cash payment in full on delivery.

When the delivery date arrived, we set up surveillance at the delivery address with two cars and a motorcycle, fully expecting to follow the delivery truck the 400 km back to its origin. The truck arrived and we immediately noticed it displayed a local license plate. It was possible that the truck had originated in our city, driven to retrieve the counterfeit products, and then returned another 400 km to make the delivery, but the hours just didn't add up. In addition, the delivery truck was in such bad condition it probably could not have endured the roundtrip.

After offloading and paying for the merchandise, our surveillance team followed the truck to a small shop sitting in front of a warehouse approximately 20 blocks from the delivery address. The driver exited the vehicle and was seen handing over the funds to an individual within the shop. The team also observed several of our client's products displayed in the shop window.

A few days later, in coordination with the police, we visited the shop and purchased two samples of our client's products, which we handed over to the police as evidence. The following day, officers executed a search warrant on the shop and adjoining warehouse. They seized several thousand counterfeit products and discovered a fully functional manufacturing facility for the counterfeits within the warehouse.

The initial online investigation was key to identifying the target and repeatedly taking down their site on the marketplace, but the organization would have continued to thrive had it not been for the actions we conducted on the ground.

Caveat Emptor

Another aspect of online marketplaces has to do with the lack of cyber safety. Many sites install malware and enable phishing scams that could damage your computer or result in loss of your personal information. This is especially true for sites that allow you to download computer software, motion pictures, music, books and other digital files.

27. Analyzing Counterfeit Products

One of the major stumbling blocks when conducting enforcement actions is the need for authorities to be certain the products they are seizing are indeed counterfeit. This involves stationing an individual during enforcement actions who can provide immediate feedback on the authenticity of a product. Without such an individual, authorities are usually reluctant to act, because they don't want to end up seizing genuine material, something that could result in a legal action against them. So, the brand owner's best interest is to provide authorities with the tools to identify counterfeit products.

In general, there are three types of tools that can assist in the authentication: written materials, specialized training and product experts.

Written materials can consist of some of the more obvious features that distinguish a genuine from a counterfeit. In the case of a sports jersey, it could be placement of the logo, color of the label, manufacturing location identified on the label and other items related to how a genuine jersey should look.

Written materials can be in printed form or accessed via what is called a How-to-Tell website available to the general public. The problem with written materials is that counterfeiters can also access the information and make the necessary changes to their products, ultimately rendering the material ineffective. It also leaves the entire process in the hands of the local authorities, who might or might not take the time or initiative to authenticate properly.

Specialized training to law enforcement and prosecutors is a valuable tool for several reasons.

• In addition to making authorities aware of the problem, training sessions allow the brand owner to explain in detail the issues involved in identifying counterfeit versus genuine products and to place the problem in context. For example, the reuse of genuine boxes and containers, giving a false impression that the contents are genuine instead of counterfeit. Or, the sale of counterfeit products to the government via the public-tender process. Or, the dangers that the counterfeits themselves pose the general public.

• Training allows the brand to teach authorities how to distinguish genuine from counterfeit products without having to educate the general public.

• Training also humanizes the brand, introducing authorities to the people behind the brand who care about the quality of their products and the reputation of their company.

• Training creates a bond between the brand owner and law enforcement, building a sense of team effort. It implies to the authorities that they will receive continued support from the brand.

• Training provides authorities with a point of contact for the brand should they need to request authentication or require further information.

The downside with training is that, with so many brands,

authorities seldom have the time to attend many training sessions, and they tend to forget all of the specifics of identifying counterfeits for every brand. So, training sessions for authorities constitute an excellent tool, but the sessions should be ongoing or their benefits are usually short-lived.

Calling in the Professionals

There is a more reliable approach: product experts. These are individuals trained by the brand holder in how to identify genuine products. They generally carry a certificate or power of attorney designating them as product experts and are qualified by the brand owner to testify in court about the authenticity of a product. In many cases, the brand owner's outside investigators will be cross-designated as product experts.

There are several benefits to this. Outside investigators are usually based in a country or city where counterfeiters of the particular product are active, so the investigators are readily available to authorities whenever they are needed. The investigators also usually speak the same language as the authorities. And the investigators tend to develop strong working ties with local authorities.

Investigators are usually experienced in participating in enforcement actions as well as dealing with both the police and prosecutors. Investigators are already the face of the client in the eyes of the authorities, so it makes a lot of sense to provide investigators with the ability to authenticate the products officially.

In some countries, however, the person authenticating the product cannot be the same as the individual swearing out the complaint. In these countries, you will need two investigators working on the case, or you need to bring in outside counsel.

I base all of the above on the premise that the manufacturer has embedded security features into its packaging to permit identification of genuine products. These measures can include RAD tags, UV ink, color-shifting ink, unique ID codes, holographic images, certificates of authenticity, security labels and other devices. Without such protection, authenticating a product can be difficult and usually requires forensic analysis by the client.

Protecting Confidentiality

If your client is training you to authenticate products, they are likely sharing trade secrets with you – secrets that if revealed to the general public or, more critically, to counterfeiters, would negate their usefulness as authentication tools. So, take great care to treat trade secrets with the highest level of confidentiality.

Yes, this is a point that should go without saying, but sometimes it can create issues with authorities. For example, law enforcement usually will ask how to determine whether a product is counterfeit or genuine. Most clients will allow you to reveal one or two telltale signs, but sometimes the counterfeits are so good that two signs are not enough. If law enforcement questions you further, and if you respond that you are not at liberty to provide further details, it can drive a wedge between you and them. They might take such a response as a lack of trust, no matter how patiently and thoroughly you explain the reasoning.

The situation can become even more difficult when dealing with an officer of the court, such as a prosecutor or a judge. Again, you might hear an argument that it is a trust issue. We have had judges go so far as threatening to order us to tell them how we determined a product was counterfeit. Whenever such a threat arose, our clients usually opted to withdraw the complaint against the counterfeiter rather than reveal trade secrets.

Keep this in mind before agreeing to take on the responsibility of learning how to authenticate your client's products.

28. To Prosecute or Not to Prosecute?

For many companies, their anti-counterfeiting strategy stops as soon as the counterfeits are removed from the market. After all, one of the major purposes of fighting counterfeits is to open up new channels to sell genuine products. Therefore, what happens to the counterfeiters after the raids and seizures tends to be of little concern. This approach, perhaps valid on paper, can be disastrous in practice.

Authorities are required by law to prosecute violators. They cannot merely seize products and ignore the violation. If authorities conduct an enforcement action at the request of a particular brand, and that brand decides not to prosecute, the authorities still must continue the process, including: taking statements and depositions, filing formal charges, storing the seized material, et cetera. If they suddenly must act without the support of the brand, the risk falls entirely on their shoulders.

As mentioned previously, many brands are vying for the attention of the authorities. If a brand leaves authorities on their own to clean up the mess following an enforcement action, how motivated do you think they will be to assist that brand in the future?

Conversely, if a brand agrees to file a complaint against the offenders, and provides product experts, samples of genuine products to compare with the counterfeit, and assists the authorities throughout the prosecution, the authorities' motivation to assist in future actions increases dramatically.

Note that the intellectual-property laws in many countries recommend incarceration only after a suspect's second or third conviction. This leaves many brand holders with the feeling of, "Why bother?" Why invest more resources into supporting the prosecution, particularly if the individual is a first-time violator? But if no one bothers to prosecute, then every counterfeiter becomes a first-time violator – over and over again.

Field Lesson 25 – Supporting law enforcement is a must

I was asked to represent one of our clients in an international training seminar, in which several brands were participating for an audience of prosecutors and law-enforcement officials from five countries. The format allotted 45 minutes to each brand to provide training and discuss their products.

The first presenter spoke about his company's strategy of using raids to bolster sales. He stressed that the sole purpose of the raids was to clear the market of counterfeits, so that buyers would be forced to purchase from legitimate dealers. He added that his company was not interested in prosecuting anyone, that their only interest was to maintain their profitability. When one of the prosecutors asked him if he was aware of what was involved in organizing a raid and of the prosecutor's obligation to press charges, the presenter responded that he understood, but that pressing charges was the prosecutor's bailiwick; the brand's only obligation was to its customers and shareholders.

The exchange did not sit well with the audience.

When it was my turn to speak, I stressed the importance of the role of the police and prosecutors in stemming the flow of counterfeit products. I related our client's philosophy of taking down organizations and not simply seizing products. I urged support for the authorities who respond to our requests for enforcement actions. I recommended providing the authorities with experts who could furnish sworn statements regarding the authenticity, or lack thereof, of the seized products. I described how we provide samples of genuine products to be used for their internal verifications. I outlined how we accompany the process by preparing sworn statements, declarations and documents as required throughout the entire process, which could stretch into years. And I set forth how we assisted authorities in destroying the counterfeit products at the end of the proceedings.

When the seminar concluded, whom do you think audience members sought out to discuss these topics? And when an enforcement action is needed, whom do you think authorities would be more eager to support?

29. The FCPA and the UK Anti-Bribery Act: Exercising Caution

Any company doing business in the United States or the United Kingdom must regard the U.S Foreign Corrupt Practices Act (FCPA) and the U.K. Anti-Bribery Act (UKABA) as gospel for all commercial and investigative actions taken abroad. There are seminars, training courses and volumes of materials written on the intricacies of both acts, but the essence boils down to a simple concept: You cannot do anything overseas that would not be permitted under U.S. or U.K. laws – even if such actions are permitted under the local laws of a particular country. This includes making facilitation payments (aka bribes) or gifts to government officials, and a broad array of additional actions.

The FCPA was established in 1977, but its enforcement has only begun to emerge over the past 10 years. In 2016, for example, the top five fines paid by U.S. companies, or companies with U.S. connections, for violating the act reached almost US$2.5 billion.[29]

UKABA is much newer, enacted in 2010.

The largest combined fine paid for violation of corruption laws was the Brazilian construction company Odebrecht, which agreed to pay fines totaling almost US$3.5 billion to the governments of Brazil, Switzerland and the United States for violations of their respective anticorruption laws.[30]

I strongly recommend that anyone conducting business overseas become intimately familiar with these important pieces of legislation, particularly because they pertain not only to you or your employees but also to your local partners and subsidiaries.

Field Lesson 26 – Ignore local laws at your peril

One of our clients learned about these important laws the hard way, when a customs broker they had hired to help secure the release of goods imported into one country paid the local customs authority to assist in facilitating the release. The broker continued to pay the same customs official over the next few years, always resulting in a swift release of the merchandise. As it turned out, in addition to our client the customs broker had amassed a long list of clients to whom he was providing similar services, none of whom was aware of the facilitation payments made on their behalf.

An internal investigation by the country's customs authorities identified the official receiving the bribes from the broker, resulting in exposure of the broker's client lists.

When our client learned about the payments, they immediately contacted U.S. authorities, volunteering all of the information and readily admitting to retaining the customs broker in question. Their cooperation resulted in some consideration by the authorities, but the client still had to pay several million U.S. dollars in fines, and they took a big hit to their reputation.

The client was so rattled by the situation that they decided to pull all operations out of that country in an attempt to avoid future violations and damage to their brand. All of this was caused by an individual not directly related to the company but rather a contractor hired to assist in handling customs paperwork.

For this reason, always be aware of your potential exposure before you conduct any activities overseas, and know your suppliers well.

30. Understanding Corporate Ethics

As important as it is to know the local and international laws and regulations, it is equally important to understand your client's corporate ethics. Simply defined, ethics are the moral principles that govern a person's or group's behavior – the principles of right and wrong. For some companies, the internal ethics and morals might be stronger than the local laws on the same subject.

Say, for example, that the laws of a particular country permit investigators to obtain photographs or videos of merchandise located in the interior of a store, as long as the store has street access and is open to the general public, and there are no postings within the store prohibiting such activity. This is the case in many countries under the premise that a store with public access can be considered public domain.

Your client might hold a different opinion, however. They might regard every building as, in essence, private property regardless of the building's use. In such cases, photographing the interior would constitute an invasion of the privacy of the store's owner or operator. Therefore, the client's ethics and morals are stricter than the laws of the country.

The same holds true on issues such as trash runs. I described earlier that trash runs can be valuable as an investigative tool, which is why they are used by law enforcement and private investigators around the world. Some clients, however, regard an individual's trash, no matter where that trash is placed, as private property. As such, going through an individual's trash would be considered an invasion of privacy – even if permitted under the law.

Other clients think it is morally wrong to investigate their own employees without first obtaining strong evidence of wrongdoing. Even when provided with substantial suspicion, the client might decide it is wrong to investigate one of their own, often opting for softer actions such as discussing the suspicions with the employee.

Such methods are usually less effective, but they fall within the moral bounds set by the client and should be respected and followed at all costs.

It is important to be thoroughly versed on the local laws and regulations, but it is equally important to know your client and understand their morals and ethics. Otherwise, you face the possibility of crossing boundaries that can result in a great deal of embarrassment for you and your client.

31. Enhancing the Value of Brand Protection

A huge dilemma faced by companies whose products are being counterfeited is whether to advertise the results of any enforcement actions. Some consumers will gain respect for a company that protects its products, and ultimately its customers, but others will lose confidence in the integrity of the brand.

For example, if a consumer learns that law enforcement has seized 500,000 counterfeit circuit breakers of X brand, representing almost half of the circuit-breaker market in a given area, the consumer might opt to purchase circuit breakers of a competing brand for fear of inadvertently purchasing a counterfeit. Likewise, if a counterfeit pain reliever resulted in an individual becoming ill, how confident would that consumer be in purchasing the same brand pain reliever to administer to their children?

How do you avoid this trap? By educating the public.

Every company with a product in danger of being counterfeit should have a system in place to ensure consumers that they are receiving genuine goods. Some companies have established hotlines that allow customers to call and verify the authenticity of products. Hotlines help consumers to feel confident in the product purchased and to receive immediate feedback if a product is counterfeit, enhancing their view of the integrity of the brand and the commitment to quality by the manufacturer.

Other companies include a How-to-tell section on their websites, including an email address allowing consumers to send inquiries about and/or photos of suspicious products. Again, this enhances the customer experience by providing a quick response to the concerns.

Another response would be to establish a network of authorized distributors, where customers can be sure they are purchasing genuine goods. The distributors are usually the company's best partners, granted favored pricing to ensure loyalty. Many companies also require their distributors to submit to unannounced audits and other measures to ensure only genuine products are sold via their facilities.

Of course, the most important part of establishing authorized distributors is providing information to the general public, making consumers aware of where to go to purchase genuine products.

In all cases, you should discuss, in advance, the decision whether or not to publish the results of enforcement actions with the client's legal team and public-relations office. At no time should the investigator be involved in making the decision or releasing information to the press. That responsibility lies solely with the client.

Another Caveat

I have seen investigators proudly display lists, and even logos, of their clients on their websites or promotional information. They might regard doing so as a great marketing tool, but you should regard it as something that does a grave disservice to the client. Clients come to investigators for assistance in resolving issues – in these cases damage to their brand caused by counterfeiting. To publicize helping the client only exposes to the world that the client has an issue – an issue that the client might not want made public. You might produce a client list to try to promote your business, but in this business doing so will not benefit your clients – and ultimately it will not benefit you.

32. Consistent Pricing and Gray Marketing

Some companies adjust their pricing location-by-location to accommodate markets in developing or underdeveloped markets, but this strategy has proven time and again to be challenging.

Lowering the price in one country only causes enterprising individuals to purchase in the cheaper market and sell in the more expensive. If, for example, a manufacturer offers an item in the United States at a price 25-percent higher than in Haiti, they inevitably will see items sold in Haiti begin to appear in the U.S. market. The upshot is that sales in Haiti will increase and sales in the United States will decrease, affecting the overall bottom line. This phenomenon is referred to as gray marketing.

Gray marketing can also involve manufacturers offering volume discounts differentially to their distributors and resellers. If the discounts are deep enough, they might see a large-scale reseller in one country, which has been moving tremendous volumes of a particular product, sell to a retail store in another country where volumes are smaller and lower dealer discounts are available. As a result, a retail store might be able to obtain the product more cheaply from a foreign distributor than from their local distributor.

Some companies consider gray marketing a routine cost of doing business globally; others see it for the problem that it is: dilution of the brand.

Interesting, but the entities hardest hit by the gray market tend to be the local distributors and partners, who see their sales and accompanying profits sinking. They often invest their own profits in advertising and sales meetings, only to have their potential clients purchase the same product at a lower price from another source. So extensive is the problem in some areas that local distributors will spend their own money to investigate the sources of gray-market products. As a result, the task of protecting the brand can sometimes be transferred to the distributor instead of the brand holder.

In addition to upsetting the price stability of products, gray marketing also affects after-sale service, which is usually funded out of local profits. If those profits decrease, and the service demands increase, this can strain a company's ability to provide service.

For example, gray-marketed products can harm a product's warranty value by forcing companies to service products not intended to be sold in a particular marketplace. Excessive warranty replacements can force a company to remove parts or products they normally keep in stock, and which they have designated to be sold at a higher price, because of the costs of replacing products sold via gray marketing.

Gray marketing can even affect a brand's image. How satisfied would you feel with a hard drive, for example, if you purchased it in an English-speaking country but discovered its instructions were in Chinese? Or, what if you purchased a food item whose nutrition values are written only in Arabic? You would likely feel that the company does not value its customers.

As potentially damaging to commerce as gray marketing can be, it is difficult to detect, particularly if the products in question are genuine and entered the country legally. In such cases, you will be unable to enlist the services of the authorities. Nevertheless, numerous tactics exist to combat gray marketing, most involving strong channel agreements and controls to ensure that products are not sold outside the primary distribution channel.

Field Lesson 27 – The value of encouraging clients to stay alert

One of our clients had become certain they were having an issue with counterfeits for the most common reason: They had witnessed a significant loss in sales over the previous six-month period in a European city, even though their products were readily available at retail locations throughout the area.

We conducted a market survey, purchasing several dozen products at prices at or below the minimum retail value for that area. Many of the products were sold in stores and retail locations outside the normal distribution network. Our client was surprised to learn that all of the purchased products were genuine. When they checked the serial numbers on the products, the numbers showed they all had originally been destined for sale in central Africa, where the suggested retail price for the product was significantly lower. It became obvious that some enterprising individuals had found an opportunity to reship the items to Europe for sale at a much higher cost – while still below the European SRP.

Working with customs, we were able to identify a series of incoming shipments of the products originating from Africa. We persuaded customs to inspect the products, but they were unable to retain them because the products were deemed genuine, and no importation laws had been violated. It was enough information, however, for the client to go back to their Central Africa distributor and pressure them into abiding by their distribution contract, threatening revocation if the issue continued.

Field Lesson 28 – Sometimes Lady Luck steps in

We were assisting one of our clients with an internal fraud investigation when we literally stumbled across a gray-market operation perpetrated by the company itself.

In the wake of a huge devaluation of the currency in one country, the local office of our client saw a significant decrease in sales. Projections for the next several quarters suggested the currency would continue to devaluate, with sales continuing their downward spiral. In an attempt to reverse the trend, an enterprising sales manager came up with a plan: sell to the neighboring countries.

The sales manager realized that devaluation had rendered the costs of genuine products in his country approximately 40-percent cheaper than across the borders. So, the client decided to sell to the neighboring countries to boost their sales.

Obviously, the plan spawned a number of issues, the most prominent of which dealt with getting the products into those neighboring countries – particularly because the brand was already represented there.

The company identified two possible routes: exporting and then importing the products through proper channels, and paying all corresponding taxes and tariffs; or simply smuggling them across the border. The legal route involved higher costs and lower profits, but because the sales manager was looking primarily to boost sales, not profits, he chose the legal route. Hence, the gray marketing.

Regarding the fact that the brand was already operating in the neighboring countries – meaning two branches of the company would be competing against each other – the sales manager chose to ignore the matter.

The upshot was that sales in the home country spiked, shooting past numbers seen even pre-devaluation. At the same time, sales in the neighboring countries tanked as cheaper versions of the genuine products smothered the market. And the overall profitability of the company declined because profits on the gray-market products were lower than what would have been earned if sold at the established prices in those countries. The whole operation dragged down the brand's value.

Remarkably, the sales manager had done nothing illegal. The exported-and-imported products complied with the laws and regulations of all countries involved. The sales manager violated no internal policies – nothing in the company guidelines prohibited selling internationally.

But was the operation ethical? Not by a long shot, although it resolved the sales manager's issue of declining revenues and even earned him a sales-based bonus. The scheme operated for almost two years before being discovered.

The lesson? This case of gray marketing by the company itself, which ate into their profits and market competitiveness, shows what kind of damage can be done by outsiders using a similar ploy.

33. Understanding the Role of Public Tenders

It might sound shocking, but some of the largest consumers of counterfeit products are governments. In most countries, as well as states and cities, governments are required to purchase supplies through a formal public-tender process, in which potential vendors bid to supply requested products at the lowest possible prices or most favorable terms.

Most individual products have an absolute bottom in terms of pricing – the lowest price offered by the company to their best distributors. This bottom is easy to identify in the public-tender process because margins are kept thin in order to win the tender. The counterfeiters need only observe the results of prior tenders to determine where that bottom lies, and then they can price their products accordingly. By pricing their products slightly lower than the genuine products, they are virtually guaranteed to win the bid.

The timing of public tenders is also advantageous to counterfeiters. When a public tender is awarded, the supplier usually has up to 120 days to deliver the products. This provides ample time for the counterfeiters to produce or purchase the counterfeits before the delivery date. Distributors of genuine products might hold the requisite inventory at the time of the bid, constituting a significant capital investment, but most counterfeiters can bid even with virtually no product on hand. They bid and begin production or place an order if and when they win the award.

The delivery margin also offers a level of security for counterfeiters, particularly those who function as distributors of counterfeits, because many times they can fill the order without ever maintaining an inventory. Take for instance printer cartridges, many of which are produced in China. The counterfeiter needs only to place the order for the counterfeits, and on their arrival and clearing customs have them delivered directly from the port to the government agency soliciting the bid – never having taken physical possession. This minimizes their risk of being caught with a container load of counterfeits.

The same holds true for medical supplies, which are often sold to public hospitals and clinics through public tenders. These agencies are interested in purchasing genuine products at the lowest possible prices, something which leaves them wide open to being supplied with counterfeit products.

Some countries are doing away with public tenders, replacing them with authorized marketplaces. Under that system, a government agency selects an authorized supplier from the marketplace and places an order. This is likewise beneficial to counterfeiters.

For one thing, because government agencies can order at will, the orders are often continuous and involve smaller quantities, thereby allowing counterfeiters to produce and/or import as needed, again without the need to maintain stock.

For another, because the authorized marketplace is accessible only to government entities, investigators are unable to conduct evidentiary purchases to support an enforcement action.

There are ways to reduce the risks of purchasing counterfeits via public tender or authorized marketplaces. These include requiring vendors to identify their suppliers and to include copies of the import documentation, if applicable. Unfortunately, most governments do not make such demands, and those that do often receive counterfeit documents.

Counterfeiters that cater their sales to the government can sometimes be the most difficult to catch. This is because most counterfeiters who participate in public tenders or authorized marketplaces do not sell to the general public, thereby making it harder for private investigators to obtain evidence to provide to prosecutors. In such cases, one of the most valuable tools is inspections. The manufacturer of the genuine product offers free inspections of items delivered during public tenders. The inspections are usually conducted by investigators trained in authenticating counterfeit products. If the items delivered turn out to be counterfeit, the investigator can then request a sample to be provided as evidence to the authorities for subsequent enforcement actions.

The inspections also benefit the receiving agency because they ensure that the products in question are genuine.

Keeping Tight Focus

This is important: Whenever you conduct an inspection, be sure to limit your comments to whether the product is genuine or not, and not how the inspection led you to that conclusion. Covert and overt security details are considered trade secrets by most manufacturers and should therefore not be disclosed to anyone without the express consent of your client. This includes comments to customers, law enforcement and even court officials.

A government agency asked us to inspect a shipment of electronics that had been purchased via public tender. Our inspection revealed that several covert features on the package were missing or altered, a clear indication of counterfeiting.

We advised the agency that 100 percent of the products we inspected were counterfeit. The official who had requested the inspection immediately asked how we were able to make that determination. We responded that we were unable to provide that information because it was a trade secret. The official excused himself for a few minutes, returning with his boss, who demanded that we provide the reasons the products were not genuine. Again, we responded that we were unable to provide this information.

The lead attorney from the agency was called in. He explained that the agency could not reject the shipment if it could not explain why the products were counterfeit. The attorney further stated that because he was an officer of the court, surely we could provide him with the information to determine that the shipment was counterfeit. Once again, we declined but stated we would be willing to sign affidavit that the products were reviewed and determined to be counterfeit.

The next morning, we were called into the office of the agency charged with overseeing public tenders. There, we were met by the head of the agency and the lead attorney. Both demanded to know how we determined that the products were counterfeit. Yet again, we explained that we could not provide this information due to our confidentiality agreement with our client. We further explained that if any of the techniques we used to determine the product's authenticity fell into the hands of the counterfeiters, they would be able to modify their packaging accordingly, severely reducing our ability to perform authentications.

The agency's attorney became irate and accused our client of failing to cooperate with the authorities to stop the spread of counterfeit products. We responded that the client was indeed committed to fighting counterfeits, which was why they had provided our authentication services free of charge to the agency. We added that we would gladly certify that an inspection had been completed and that the products in question were determined to be counterfeit. But under no circumstances would we divulge how we had reached this determination.

The attorney calmed down. He and his boss realized that we were offering to inspect products at no cost whenever needed and to document the results of the inspection – actions that relieved the agency of responsibility for determining whether they were buying genuine products. We eventually became strong allies of the agency, and they became a reliable source of investigative leads for companies selling counterfeit products of our client's brand through the public-tender system.

34. Avoid Becoming an Evidence Custodian

It is unthinkable for a U.S. or European private investigator to become an evidence custodian for merchandise seized on behalf of the client, but in many countries around the world it is a common practice.

Prosecutors and police often lack the space to store seized items, much less the security to ensure that the products and their integrity remain intact. Therefore, in many countries, it is common for the investigator or attorney to store the seized items until trial or until the products are no longer required by the court. It is common, but there are reasons why no investigator should ever consider taking on this responsibility.

First, it is a conflict of interest. The investigator can never be seen as an impartial party when representing their client, particularly if they were heavily involved in identifying and coordinating the seizure of the counterfeits. A smart defense attorney would easily claim that the products were switched or tampered with while under the control of the investigator.

Second, it is a liability. If anything befalls the evidence, the investigator would be held personally responsible. This includes not only tampering but also theft and damage if the products were stolen or missing. The same holds true for damage of any sort to the products, including water, fire, humidity or even insects. Not only would it be an issue for trial, but it also could encourage the court to order that the products be returned to the owner or restitution made.

Third, there is the whole financial side. In many countries, a trial can take several years. At any given time while awaiting the trial, the client could opt to back out of the case for any number of reasons. The client might change the IP enforcement strategy or even file for bankruptcy. Likewise, the client might no longer sell the items in question or lose interest as the items become outdated. If any of these possibilities developed, the evidence custodian would still be required to maintain safe control over the seized items through the end of the case – with no reimbursement for costs.

So, any way you slice it, an investigator should never agree to become an evidence custodian.

35. Working with Authorities

Seeking assistance from authorities to conduct enforcement actions is not always an easy task, particularly when operating overseas where sometimes multinational corporations are viewed as taking advantage of the people, and counterfeiting is seen as a way for the little guy to get by.

Likewise, if the big bad multinational loses profits, it is not considered an injustice because they are viewed as rolling in money. Nevertheless, with persistence and a little understanding of what makes the authorities tick, there is usually a way to persuade them to carry out the actions.

Field Lesson 30 – Sometimes it pays to go to the top

While representing a major technology company with counterfeit issues in a country in Latin America, we had planned several raids we could not execute because of corruption and even a general lack of interest by the authorities. Attempting to remedy the situation, I requested and received an invitation to meet with the country's Minister of Interior to determine the best method to proceed.

After explaining that we had unsuccessfully attempted enforcement actions against numerous targets selling counterfeits of our client's brand, the minister sympathized. But he added that, from the administration's perspective, attacking counterfeits was bad for the country's economy – counterfeiting had created jobs for the underprivileged who had no other means of earning a living.

The minister asked what my client would do to compensate the poor people that would be put out of business if he authorized enforcement actions. I respectfully responded that social programs were the responsibility of the government, not the private sector, and I reminded the minister that no taxes were being paid on counterfeit goods – money which could be used to fund social programs to help the underprivileged.

The debate lasted nearly three hours and ranged from the minister's position that poverty was created by large corporations overcharging for everyday goods, to his suggestion that the multinationals offer to sell their genuine products to the counterfeiters at a reduced rate to incentivize them not to counterfeit, to the request that my client set up a fund to train the counterfeiters in some type of trade that would allow them to find alternate employment.

Toward the end, where it appeared that we would not be able to come to an agreement, the minister confided that he harbored ambitions to become president of his country someday. I told him that if he would cooperate with the enforcement actions, we would thank his office publicly for their support, giving him a plaque and a letter signed by the CSO of my client's company praising the minister's assistance, all at a venue of the minister's choice. I also agreed to advise the U.S. Embassy of his cooperation because our client was a U.S. company. I added that we would arrange for media to be present at the moment of the raid, so the minister could claim the action as the first step in his nation's fight against intellectual-property violations.

At that point, the minister agreed to conduct the enforcement actions. In fact, the minister became so agreeable that he expanded the scope of the actions to include a variety of violations in addition to counterfeiting.

The following week, the authorities executed search warrants against eight major targets for violations including counterfeiting, tax evasion, tax fraud, immigration violations and even sanitary and safety infractions. The authorities even went so far as to charge the owners of the shopping center with conspiracy, alleging they were aware of the violations within their premises but did nothing to prevent them.

The raids resulted in the seizure of over US$1 million in counterfeit items, the equivalent of hundreds of thousands more in fines for tax evasion, the temporary closing of two of the shops for sanitary and safety purposes and the arrest of more than a dozen foreigners working and living illegally, one of whom was a fugitive from his home country wanted by Interpol.

The minister arrived toward the end of the enforcement action. He enjoyed his so-called 15 minutes of fame

in front of the media and the TV cameras. Ultimately, the minister failed to win his party's nomination and never realized his dream of running for president, but he did keep his word to assist our anti-counterfeiting actions.

Not every local or national official wants to be president, but there are usually ways to nudge those in a position to assist with enforcement actions without violating any laws or regulations, including the FCPA and the U.K. Anti-Bribery Act. For example, providing a plaque or other commendation to both the chief of police and the head of the police unit assisting with the investigation can go a long way. A letter of commendation from you or your client can also assist the advancement of the officer's career. Even something as minimal as allowing the officer to take full credit for an investigation you developed and ran can greatly – and legally – strengthen your relationship with an official in a position to help you.

36. Dealing with Clients

Though not specifically part of the investigative process, it is necessary to be somewhat vague when providing investigative proposals to clients.

I have learned this the hard way.

Field Lesson 31 – Sometimes clients can outsmart themselves

Several years ago, we were asked to meet with a client whose line of footwear had recently been counterfeited widely. After laying out the problem in detail, the company asked us to submit a proposal outlining the steps we would take to reduce the number of counterfeits on the market. The client requested that the proposal be as detailed as possible, explaining this was their first experience with counterfeits and that they would need to present the proposal to the company's board of directors.

Following the client's instructions, we prepared a detailed proposal with associated fees for conducting each of the outlined steps. We presented the proposal, following up with a call a few days later to see if they had any questions. The client responded that the board was spread out geographically, so it would take a few weeks for to complete their review and advise us of their decision.

Approximately two months later, I received a call from the client, asking me to meet at their offices. The following morning, I met the president and general manager, who informed me they were pleased with the strategy we had outlined. Then they informed me that they had already completed the first two steps of the plan on their own but were having trouble figuring out how to conduct the third step.

I informed them that our proposal was designed for us to conduct the investigative steps, but if the client preferred to investigate in-house, we could act as consultants, assisting them with planning and executing the remainder of the strategy. But the client was not interested in a consultancy agreement – if we could just help with the third step, they would continue on their own. Needless to say, we refused.

About a year later, the client contacted us again, admitting they had not been able to move forward with the investigation, and the company had reached a critical stage. The market had changed, new competitors entered the scene and their reputation was severely damaged due to the flood of counterfeits. They asked us to devise a new strategy and submit a proposal. We did, this time keeping the details of the strategy to ourselves. Unfortunately, the company closed shortly thereafter as a result of their widespread counterfeit problem.

37. Building an Anti-Counterfeiting Program

Given the realities of today's global economy, it is inevitable that successful companies selling consumer products will experience counterfeiting. It might occur in the early stages of their business, perhaps while they are introducing an innovative product, or possibly at a later stage as the brand matures and gains market share. Either way, at some point it will happen. As the famed English writer Charles Caleb Colter stated in the early 1800's, "imitation is the sincerest form of flattery." So, businesses must be prepared to handle this unique form of commercial flattery.

When the time comes, you will need to design a successful anti-counterfeiting program, the specifics of which will depend largely on the nature of the product and industry. But the overall structure of the program will remain essentially the same.

A successful anti-counterfeiting program should contain, at a minimum, four major components, to which we refer using the acronym PETE:

- Prevention measures
- Enforcement activities
- Training
- Education

Prevention measures include significant design features on the products themselves or packaging, making them difficult to copy. Also included are overt security features such as security labels, bar codes, QR codes and RFI tags, as well as other items designed to easily identify and track genuine products throughout the distribution channel, as well as covert features for these same purposes that are not easily identifiable by consumers or counterfeiters. All are designed to ensure the integrity of the product from its manufacturing stage through purchase by the end user.

Enforcement measures involve everything I have explained in this book. They include investigations and efforts, both online and on the ground, designed to identify the companies or individuals manufacturing, importing and/or distributing counterfeit goods, and coordinating with local authorities to remove those items from the market as expeditiously as possible. This is the most critical – and expensive – component of the strategy, because it is impossible to employ an effective strategy if it lacks a significant deterrent factor.

Training authorities is likewise essential, because it enables governments to deal more effectively with the problems faced by the brand holders. Training provides authorities with the informational tools they need to identify the genuine from the counterfeit. Training also establishes a face for your client and gives the authorities a means to contact them when they identify counterfeit products or when they need assistance with the brand.

Education provides end users with the means to determine that the products they have acquired are genuine. In addition, education informs the client why it is important to offer a genuine product, not a cheaper imitation. You can also use education to show how counterfeiting operations often employ sweatshops, child labor and connections with other illegal activities. Another important element of education is reminding end users where they can purchase genuine products, such as lists of authorized distributors or stores approved by the manufacturer.

These four components form the basis of an effective anti-counterfeiting program. As you proceed, you can add more items to augment the effort, but these represent the minimum requirements needed for success.

As a caveat to the above, an important sub-component to enforcement measures is a system to generate and store intelligence that will support enforcement measures, such as the names of individuals, companies and markets; their telephone numbers and addresses, and other information gathered during your investigations. Such intelligence over time will help you identify groups and organizations involved in counterfeiting your clients' products, as well as their *modi operandi*.

As your program matures and your intelligence database grows, you will be able to identify more effectively the connections between organizations operating in different regions or countries, and your investigations will become more intelligence-driven, instead of being reactive to the discovery of a counterfeiting problem.

• An intelligence-driven program will allow you to target individuals involved in counterfeiting instead of always chasing after counterfeit products.

• An intelligence-driven program will allow you to target different areas within an organization to dismantle the entire operation instead of obtaining a simple seizure.

• An intelligence-driven program will allow you to take out major distributors of components that are supplying multiple organizations, effectively crippling those organizations.

• An intelligence-driven program is more efficient and effective than a reactive program – but it requires a significant investment in the collection of information for future analysis.

POSTSCRIPT

I have attempted to focus this book on the enforcement side of fighting counterfeiting, but the truth of the matter is that law enforcement, industry and private investigators cannot stop the problem on their own. As with illegal drugs, counterfeiting will continue as long as there is a demand for the counterfeit products. As long as someone is willing to shell out the money to purchase a counterfeit product, those products will continue to exist despite the best efforts of all involved in trying to stop them.

What, then, is the missing piece of the puzzle? Demand reduction. Industry and the government must find a way to discourage the public from seeking, and purchasing, counterfeit products. Because we're talking about basic human behavior and urges, reducing the demand is the most difficult part of the equation.

Another problem: In some cases, demand is not the issue. Take for example counterfeit medicines. Obviously, no one wants to purchase phony medications. Everyone wants the genuine product – many people are leery of even generic alternatives – in hopes of curing whatever ailments have afflicted them. No, buying counterfeit meds is most often a price issue. Nevertheless, the buyer is taking a big risk, and the counterfeiter is the willing partner. Retailers sometimes get involved as well. Clinics or pharmacies trying to shave a few points from their bottom line might opt for the cheapest alternative, paying no regards to the product's origin or authenticity. Again, it doesn't mean the end-user desires such products.

The urge to save money applies in other cases as well. Take, for example, a circuit breaker or an engine part that isn't readily visible. Many consumers, looking to fix an issue in the cheapest way possible and without thinking of the potential consequences, will simply opt for the cheapest alternative without considering the possibility that it is counterfeit. They are not interested in buying a specific brand so much as solving an immediate problem on the cheap. As long as the replacement appears to work and the price is good, the buyer might not give the action a second thought.

Class Envy

Regarding designer handbags or other fashion items, on the other hand, chances are that the person buying a counterfeit is entirely aware of what is transpiring. Anyone who buys a US$2000 handbag for a couple of hundred dollars – or less – knows it is a fake. It becomes purely a question of wanting to create the impression of owning a designer product – feeding status-consciousness – but being unable or unwilling to pay full price. The buyer feeds personal insecurities while feeling little concern that child labor probably helped manufacture the handbag. Or that part of the purchase price is destined for criminal organizations involved in a myriad of illegal activities such as drug trafficking, prostitution, extortion and human trade.

Worse, funds from counterfeit purchases might be destined for terrorist activities. The consumer gives very little thought to these activities. The desire for immediate gratification overcomes any pangs of conscience.

Fighting Temptations with Facts

Back to the cases of counterfeit medicines. I have found that the most effective way to reduce demand for fake meds is to punish, severely, those who choose to manufacture and distribute them. The enforcement actions we have been discussing in this book, coupled with lobbying for stricter laws to punish those preying on unsuspecting consumers, can go a long way toward wiping out counterfeit pharmaceuticals.

That is the starting point. Next, we need to do a better job of educating the public about how and where to buy reliable and genuine products – at least, on the consumer end. If consumers are already purchasing from what they deem to be genuine distributors – hospitals, pharmacies, clinics, et cetera – we need to concentrate on the retailers who might be tempted to mislead them. Here, the odds are on our side, because most consumers always want genuine medicines.

Where counterfeit engine parts are concerned, education likewise can go a long way to reduce demand for counterfeits. If we can persuade, say, purchasers of automotive parts that there is always danger in trusting a counterfeit – the possibility of brake failure, sudden airbag deployment or engine seizing, for examples – more would be inclined to make sure they have purchased genuine parts.

The same for counterfeit circuit breakers that could cause fires. If we can make clear and spread widely the concept that fake products can be dangerous, we increase the chances that consumers will always seek the genuine articles. The flipside to this, of course, is always to make sure consumers are aware of where they can buy the genuine goods, perhaps through a well-defined network of official distributors.

Looking again at counterfeit designer apparel, consumers so often make such purchases based on emotion – how they would feel holding a designer handbag; how they would look wearing designer jeans or a particular style of footwear, how they would like to own something similar to a famous entertainer or person they might admire.

The problem we professionals face in fighting fashion counterfeiters is they create no immediate dangers to consumers seeking their product, so it becomes difficult to encourage consumers to resist those particular temptations. We are left with attempting to remind consumers how the products were manufactured – in the sweatshops, using child labor, in unhealthy work environments –

and how the products probably were smuggled into the country by individuals who also traffic in illegal drugs, weapons and human beings, not to mention the use of some of the proceeds to fund other criminal activities as well as terrorism, and the fact that purchases of knockoffs mean loss of jobs for honest workers and less tax revenues.

All-in-all, it can be a daunting task, particularly given that each consumer is different, and what appeals to one might not attract another. Nevertheless, the challenge should not be overlooked. If such approaches comprise even a single part of a company's anti-counterfeiting strategy, and if they result in, say, a 5-percent reduction in counterfeiting, that translates into a substantial savings – and a hit to a criminal organization.

Most important, as in drug-trafficking, any counterfeiting reductions can be extremely gratifying when they result in less exploitation of children. Speaking of which, if children are taught from a young age that downloading a song from a P2P site is wrong, that replacing a chip in a gaming console so that copied games can be played is wrong, that hacking into the protection software on a digital book to make a copy is wrong, then the struggles against counterfeiting in the future would stand a much better chance of success.

PART IV: My Story

MY INTEREST IN INVESTIGATIONS first appeared at a young age
– you might even say I was born into it. My father was a federal
agent for over 30 years, first with the Border Patrol, part of what is
now called the U.S. Customs and Border Protection Agency, then
with the Internal Revenue Service, which he followed by joining
the Bureau of Narcotics and Dangerous Drugs – today the Drug
Enforcement Administration.

I grew up with the investigation bug in my blood. After gradu-
ating from college, I tried different jobs such as teaching languages,
working in the food industry and selling different products. But
in the end, all were means of buying time until my background
investigation was completed with the DEA.

I joined the agency in 1987 in their Denver Field Division,
and for the next 15 years of my life I spent close to every waking
moment chasing drug dealers throughout the United States and
Latin America. I covered a wide range of assignments, from deci-
phering the high-frequency radio transmissions of drug traffickers
in Northern Colombia to participating in the invasion of Panama in search of evidence against Manuel Antonio Noriega, that
country's de facto dictator at the time. I was involved in identifying and knocking down drug labs in Peru, mapping out clandes-
tine airstrips in Argentina and uncovering cocaine organizations
in Bolivia. And I oversaw intelligence for DEA's largest field division covering Florida and the Caribbean. I worked on some of the
largest seizures of drugs transiting from the southern portion of
South America – and everywhere in between.

In 2002, I was working in DEA's office in La Paz, Bolivia, in
charge of the Intelligence Unit and covering five South American

countries. Shortly after arriving, my family was forced to move to Santa Cruz, almost 400 miles to the east, because my infant son suffered breathing difficulties in La Paz's thin air, some 13,500 feet above sea level.

Making a Transition

Unhappy with being separated from my family, and somewhat burnt out from working drugs, I began looking for a change. As luck would have it, I was contacted by a Microsoft representative who was looking for someone to fill the position of investigator for the Latin American division. The position was initially to be based out of São Paulo, but after going through a series of interviews, my new employers agreed to allow me to work at the Microsoft Latin America offices in Fort Lauderdale, Florida.

I was excited to make the switch from government service to private practice, but in retrospect I realize I was naïve in thinking my skills could transfer seamlessly. I also was ignorant about the intricacies of intellectual-property investigations, thinking that my entire job would be seizing counterfeit products.

One of the first lessons I learned was that the investigative budget for chasing counterfeiters is nowhere near the budget we had at DEA for chasing drug dealers. Equally important, though it could take years to bring a drug investigation to successful completion, anything more than a month or so on the corporate side was not considered productive.

I spent the next two years learning the trade and running some interesting and successful cases. One investigation resulted in shutting down an entire shopping center dedicated to the sale of counterfeit software for four weeks and charging the owners with conspiracy to commit fraud, something that had never been done before in that country.

Another investigation led to the discovery of a solid connection between a group of counterfeiters and a well-known terrorist organization, something that had only been the subject of speculation until then. Yet another investigation led to the recovery of over US$1-million in back taxes by a chain of retail stores selling counterfeit goods and defrauding the government.

I truly enjoyed my time at Microsoft, but I slowly concluded that I could do a better job than many of the outside investigators I had been hiring. So, in 2003, with our two young boys in tow, my wife and I moved to Argentina, and set up our company.

Private Practice

MIC Worldwide was born in August 2003 with two owner / employees, one client and high hopes. That client was Microsoft, which agreed to give us the equivalent of 20 hours per week in fees for six months to conduct investigations for them in the Southern Cone of South America. We felt incredibly grateful to Microsoft for the opportunity, so we each jumped in with both feet to meet their goals. Three months later we signed a second client, then a third and things slowly snowballed from there.

Our first office was the balcony of our small apartment. We enclosed the 6-feet-by-3-feet space, and my wife and I worked back-to-back during the first six months. As the business grew, we rented an apartment in the same building and hired on our first employees. A couple of years later, we moved into a professional office building, and later opened additional offices in Miami and Paraguay, hiring more employees.

After 15 Years

My passion for investigations continues as strong as ever. I still get the same rush when opening a container of counterfeit products as I did back when we were seizing shipments of cocaine. I still enjoy piecing the puzzle together from start, trying to outsmart the counterfeiters at every turn. I like helping clients develop their anti-counterfeiting strategies and setting our goals, and then surpassing the client's expectations. I enjoy the interaction with local authorities and the negotiations involved in persuading them to support our efforts. I enjoy representing our clients through training and speaking events. I enjoy the challenge. I enjoy the chase. But most of all, I enjoy the fact that every day is different. As much as investigations can be similar, no two are exactly alike, which makes this life and business endlessly interesting.

For those of you who will choose or have chosen this path, I wish you success.

Appendix 1

The World's Most Valuable Branded Products

Source: Forbes – as of October 30, 2018

Rank	Brand	Value (USD)	Brand Revenue (USD)
1	Apple	$182.8 B	$228.6 B
2	Google	$132.1 B	$97.2 B
3	Microsoft	$104.9 B	$98.4 B
4	Facebook	$94.8 B	$35.7 B
5	Amazon	$70.9 B	$169.3 B
6	Coca-Cola	$53.7 B	$23.4 B
7	Samsung	$47.6 B	$203.4 B
8	Disney	$47.5 B	$30.4 B
9	Toyota	$44.7 B	$176.4 B
10	AT&T	$41.9 B	$160.5 B
11	McDonald's	$41.4 B	$90.9 B
12	GE	$37.2 B	$104.9 B
13	Mercedes-Benz	$34.4 B	$116.9 B
14	Intel	$34.1 B	$62.8 B
15	Louis Vuitton	$33.6 B	$12.9 B
16	Cisco	$32.4 B	$48.1 B
17	IBM	$32.1 B	$79.1 B
18	Nike	$32.0 B	$33.3 B
19	Verizon	$31.4 B	$126.0 B
20	BMW	$31.4 B	$86.8 B
21	Oracle	$30.8 B	$39.5 B
22	Marlboro	$26.6 B	n/a
23	SAP	$26.2 B	$25.4 B
24	Honda	$25.5 B	$120.4 B
25	Budweiser	$25.5 B	$11.6 B
26	Walmart	$24.9 B	$335.5 B
27	Visa	$24.5 B	$18.4 B
28	American Express	$23.1 B	$35.6 B
29	Pepsi	$18.4 B	$9.7 B
30	L'Oréal	$17.2 B	$10.1 B
31	Nescafe	$17.1 B	$9.1 B
32	Gillette	$17.1 B	$6.6 B
33	Home Depot	$16.4 B	$100.9 B
34	Starbucks	$16.2 B	$21.9 B
35	Hermes	$15.3 B	$6.0 B

Rank	Brand	Value (USD)	Brand Revenue (USD)
36	Gucci	$14.9 B	$6.7 B
37	Audi	$14.8 B	$59.1 B
38	Accenture	$14.8 B	$39.1 B
39	ESPN	$14.6 B	$11.4 B
40	IKEA	$14.5 B	$39.3 B
41	Frito-Lay	$14.4 B	$11.4 B
42	Ford	$14.1 B	$149.3 B
43	Wells Fargo	$13.5 B	$97.7 B
44	UPS	$13.3 B	$65.9 B
45	CVS	$13.2 B	$184.8 B
46	Zara	$13.0 B	$18.9 B
47	H&M	$13.0 B	$22.5 B
48	Siemens	$12.8 B	$90.0 B
49	Mastercard	$12.4 B	$12.5 B
50	HP	$12.4 B	$80.9 B
51	J.P. Morgan	$11.9 B	$47.4 B
52	HSBC	$11.9 B	$76.6 B
53	Nestle	$11.7 B	$8.6 B
54	Fox	$11.7 B	$16.3 B
55	Netflix	$11.5 B	$11.7 B
56	Chevrolet	$11.5 B	$81.0 B
57	Pampers	$11.4 B	$8.5 B
58	Porsche	$11.0 B	$25.5 B
59	Cartier	$10.6 B	$6.3 B
60	Bank of America	$10.4 B	$81.7 B
61	Red Bull	$10.4 B	$6.8 B
62	Ebay	$10.3 B	$8.6 B
63	Sony	$10.2 B	$62.8 B
64	Chase	$10.2 B	$55.1 B
65	Citi	$10.1 B	$88.0 B
66	Colgate	$10.0 B	$5.3 B
67	Danone	$10.0 B	$10.6 B
68	Adidas	$9.5 B	$20.6 B
69	Lexus	$9.5 B	$20.7 B
70	Nissan	$9.4 B	$95.2 B
71	Rolex	$9.3 B	$4.6 B
72	T-Mobile	$9.0 B	$38.7 B
73	Kraft	$8.8 B	$6.5 B

Rank	Brand	Value (USD)	Brand Revenue (USD)
74	Corona	$8.8 B	$5.7 B
75	Hyundai	$8.7 B	$81.8 B
76	Santander	$8.7 B	$49.5 B
77	BASF	$8.6 B	$69.9 B
78	Lowe's	$8.5 B	$68.6 B
79	Huawei	$8.4 B	$85.9 B
80	Adobe	$8.3 B	$7.3 B
81	FedEx	$8.3 B	$63.9 B
82	Heineken	$8.2 B	$5.6 B
83	Goldman Sachs	$8.2 B	$42.3 B
84	Kellogg's	$8.2 B	$5.8 B
85	Boeing	$8.1 B	$93.4 B
86	Costco	$8.0 B	$136.0 B
87	Chanel	$8.0 B	$5.6 B
88	Lancome	$8.0 B	$5.3 B
89	Nivea	$7.9 B	$4.7 B
90	Volkswagen	$7.9 B	$99.6 B
91	LEGO	$7.8 B	$5.1 B
92	Panasonic	$7.8 B	$68.4 B
93	Philips	$7.7 B	$26.8 B
94	RBC	$7.7 B	$37.4 B
95	Allianz	$7.6 B	$118.7 B
96	Uniqlo	$7.5 B	$13.0 B
97	Walgreens	$7.5 B	$84.7 B
98	PayPal	$7.5 B	$13.1 B
99	Dell	$7.5 B	$76.8 B
100	KFC	$7.4B	$24.5 B

Appendix 2
Selected Treaties Administered by the
U.N. World Intellectual Property Organization

• Beijing Treaty on Audiovisual Performances (adopted in 2012) – deals with the intellectual-property rights of audiovisual performances. An audiovisual performance is defined as an event of sound and image manipulation.

• Berne Convention for the Protection of Literary and Artistic Works (1886) – deals with the protection of works and rights of authors, musicians, poets, painters and others.

• Brussels Satellite Convention (1974) – requires each contracting state to take adequate measures to prevent unauthorized distribution on or from its territory of any program-carrying signal transmitted by satellite.

• Madrid Agreement Concerning the International Registration of Marks (1891) – states that "all goods bearing a false or deceptive indication of source, by which one of the contracting states, or a place situated therein, is directly or indirectly indicated as being the country or place of origin, must be seized on importation, or such importation must be prohibited, or other actions and sanctions must be applied in connection with such importation."

• Marrakesh VIP Treaty (2013) – forms part of the body of the international copyright treaties administered by WIPO. Contains a clear humanitarian and social development dimension with the main goal of creating a set of mandatory limitations and exceptions for the benefit of the blind, visually impaired and otherwise print disabled.

• Nairobi Treaty on the Protection of the Olympic Symbol (1981) – requires all signatories to protect the Olympic symbol against use for commercial purposes without the authorization of the International Olympic Committee.

- Paris Convention for the Protection of Industrial Property (1883) – applies to industrial property in the widest sense, including patents, trademarks, industrial designs, utility models, service marks, trade names, geographical indications and the repression of unfair competition. This international agreement was the first major step taken to help creators ensure that their intellectual works were protected in other countries.

- Patent Law Treaty (2000) – intended to harmonize and streamline formal procedures regarding national and regional patent applications and patents, and making such procedures more user-friendly.

- Phonograms Convention (1971) – requires each contracting state to protect a producer of phonograms who is a national of another contracting state against making duplicates without that producer's consent, to protect against the importation of such duplicates where the making or importation is for the purpose of distribution to the public, and to protect against the distribution of such duplicates to the public.

- Rome Convention for the Protection of Performers, Producers of Phonograms and Broadcasting Organizations (1961) – secures protection in performances for performers, in phonograms for producers of phonograms and in broadcasts for broadcasting organizations.

- Singapore Treaty on the Law of Trademarks (2006) – creates a modern and dynamic international framework to harmonize administrative trademark registration procedures.

- Trademark Law Treaty (1994) – intended to standardize and streamline national and regional trademark-registration procedures.

- Washington Treaty (1989) – protects the layout designs (topographies) of integrated circuits. The treaty has not yet entered into force but has been ratified or acceded to by Bosnia and Herzegovina, Egypt and Saint Lucia.

• WIPO Copyright Treaty (1996) – a special agreement under the Berne Convention (see above), which grants certain economic rights and deals with two subject matters to be protected by copyright: computer programs, whatever the mode or form of their expression, and compilations of data or other material (databases).

• WIPO Performance and Phonogram Treaty (1996) – deals with the rights of two types of beneficiaries, particularly in the digital environment: performers (actors, singers, musicians, et cetera) and producers of phonograms (persons or legal entities responsible for the fixation of sounds).

One other important piece of legislation is the 2011 Anti-Counterfeiting Trade Agreement (ACTA), which provides international standards for enforcing IP rights and targets counterfeit trade-marked goods, counterfeit generic medicines and pirated copyrighted material.[31]

Acknowledgments

WRITING THIS BOOK turned out to be longer and more intense experience than I had anticipated. And though my name is on the cover of the book, a lot of people worked behind the scenes to make it happen.

First and foremost, I would like to thank my beautiful wife Dafne, whose idea it was for me to write this book in the first place. Dafne is also responsible for the concept of adding true experiences as learning tools – the Field Lessons – making the book far more readable than the bland instruction manual I began writing many months ago. Without her encouragement and gentle prodding, this book would have never come to being.

Many thanks to Ron Davis who wrote the Foreword. Ron is a true icon and leader in the intellectual-property field, and I am deeply honored that he took time out from his busy schedule to contribute to this effort.

I would like to thank my editor, Phil Berardelli, whose patience and constant coaching kept me going when no end was in sight.

I would also like to thank our clients who have trusted us to protect their brands. We never take this trust lightly. Each brand is unique, and every case represents a new challenge and learning experience. We remain constantly grateful for the chance to contribute to the success and health of our clients' brands.

Last, I would like to thank the investigators, too many to name, with whom I have come in contact throughout my career, in both the private and public sectors. True investigators share their successes, as well as failures, with one other, and all constitute invaluable learning experiences. Through this sharing, we all grow as investigators, and I am grateful and indebted to each and every one of you.

End Notes

1. "PwC survey shows global R&D spending on all-time high," DW.com, October 24, 2017.
2. Seth Grodin, "Define: Brand," Seth's Blog, SethGodin.typepad.com, December 13, 2009.
3. Amazon.com keyword search: "brand value."
4. "The World's Most Valuable Brands, 2018 Ranking," Forbes.com.
5. Kurt Badenhausen, "The World's Most Valuable Brands 2018: By The Numbers," Forbes.com, May 23, 2018.
6. "Global Brand Counterfeiting Report, 2018," ResearchandMarkets. com.
7. "Fake products cost 800,000 jobs annually," European Economic and Social Committee, eesc.europa.eu, July 18, 2017.
8. "Global Cost of Counterfeiting Is $1.8 Trillion, According to New Netnames Report," IndustryToday.com, Vol. 10, Issue 14, 2015.
9. Udo Pfleghar and Steffen Schäffner, "The costs of counterfeiting: an exemplary study of the pharmaceutical industry, WorldTrade-markReview.com, May 18, 2017.
10. IndustryToday.com, op. cit.
11. Don-Alvin Adegeest, "Global counterfeiting costs luxury brands billions of dollars," FashionUnited.uk, ⅞AY 19, 2018.
12. IndustryToday.com, op. cit.
13. Glenn Taylor, "90% of Online Businesses Experience Revenue Loss Due to Counterfeit Sales," RetailTouchPoints.com, January 11, 2016.
14. Leticia Miranda and Megha Rajagopalan, "Small American businesses are struggling against a flood of Chinese fakes," BuzzFeed News via CNBC.com.
15. Ibid.
16. Glenn Taylor, op. cit.
17. Air Bags," U.S. National Highway Traffic Safety Administration, NHTSA.gov.
18. "Vehicles in operation in the United States – Statistics & Facts," Statista.com.
19. "An Unnerving Reality," AerospaceManufacturingandDesign.com, February 2009.

20. Stijn Hoorens, "The Costs of Counterfeiting," The RAND Blog, November 28, 2012.

21. IndustryToday.com, op. cit.

22. IndustryToday.com, op. cit.

23. Zayani Bhatt, "The medical industry's newest problem – counterfeit medical devices," MIMS Today, June 21, 2017.

24. ie Thibault, "Hackers Flock to Fake Medical Devices," MDDIonline.com, September 30, 2015.

25. Anti-Counterfeiting Trade Agreement (ACTA), Office of the United States Trade Representative.

26. The International Anti-Counterfeiting Coalition, Inc.

27. Statement by U.S. Trade Representative Robert Lighthizer on Section 301 Action, July 10, 2018.

28. Anna Giaritelli, "Feds seize $500 million worth of fake designer goods in black market sting operations," Washington Examiner, August 16, 2018.

29. 2017 Year-End FCPA Update, Gibson Dunn, January 2, 2018.

30. "Odebrecht and Braskem Plead Guilty and Agree to Pay at Least $3.5 Billion in Global Penalties to Resolve Largest Foreign Bribery Case in History," U.S. Department of Justice Office of Public Affairs, December 21, 2016.

31. Anti-Counterfeiting Trade Agreement (ACTA), Office of the United States Trade Representative, op. cit.

Made in the USA
Coppell, TX
13 September 2020

37744810R00085